AJAX PROGRAMMING

CREATE POWERFUL WEB AND MOBILE APPLICATIONS

4 BOOKS IN 1

BOOK 1
AJAX PROGRAMMING FOR BEGINNERS: BUILDING DYNAMIC WEB
INTERFACES

BOOK 2
INTERMEDIATE AJAX TECHNIQUES: ENHANCING USER EXPERIENCE AND
PERFORMANCE

BOOK 3
ADVANCED AJAX STRATEGIES: SCALABLE SOLUTIONS FOR COMPLEX WEB
APPLICATIONS

BOOK 4
MASTERING AJAX: ARCHITECTING ROBUST WEB AND MOBILE SOLUTIONS

ROB BOTWRIGHT

Published by Rob Botwright
Library of Congress Cataloging-in-Publication Data
ISBN 978-1-83938-731-9
Cover design by Rizzo

Disclaimer

The contents of this book are based on extensive research and the best available historical sources. However, the author and publisher make no claims, promises, or guarantees about the accuracy, completeness, or adequacy of the information contained herein. The information in this book is provided on an "as is" basis, and the author and publisher disclaim any and all liability for any errors, omissions, or inaccuracies in the information or for any actions taken in reliance on such information. The opinions and views expressed in this book are those of the author and do not necessarily reflect the official policy or position of any organization or individual mentioned in this book. Any reference to specific people, places, or events is intended only to provide historical context and is not intended to defame or malign any group, individual, or entity. The information in this book is intended for educational and entertainment purposes only. It is not intended to be a substitute for professional advice or judgment. Readers are encouraged to conduct their own research and to seek professional advice where appropriate. Every effort has been made to obtain necessary permissions and acknowledgments for all images and other copyrighted material used in this book. Any errors or omissions in this regard are unintentional, and the author and publisher will correct them in future editions.

BOOK 1 - AJAX PROGRAMMING FOR BEGINNERS: BUILDING DYNAMIC WEB INTERFACES

BOOK 2 - INTERMEDIATE AJAX TECHNIQUES: ENHANCING USER EXPERIENCE AND PERFORMANCE

BOOK 3 - ADVANCED AJAX STRATEGIES: SCALABLE SOLUTIONS FOR COMPLEX WEB APPLICATIONS

BOOK 4 - MASTERING AJAX: ARCHITECTING ROBUST WEB AND MOBILE SOLUTIONS

Introduction

Welcome to the AJAX Programming book bundle, where you'll embark on an exciting journey to master the art of creating powerful web and mobile applications using Asynchronous JavaScript and XML (AJAX). This comprehensive bundle consists of four distinct books, each carefully crafted to cater to developers of all skill levels, from beginners to seasoned professionals.

In Book 1, "AJAX Programming for Beginners: Building Dynamic Web Interfaces," you'll dive into the fundamentals of AJAX programming. Starting with the basics of asynchronous requests and server communication, you'll learn how to build dynamic web interfaces that respond seamlessly to user interactions. Through hands-on tutorials and practical examples, beginners will gain the essential skills needed to kickstart their journey into AJAX development.

Moving forward, Book 2, "Intermediate AJAX Techniques: Enhancing User Experience and Performance," delves deeper into intermediate-level AJAX concepts. Here, you'll explore advanced techniques aimed at enhancing user experience and optimizing application performance. From error handling to caching strategies, this book equips developers with the tools to create faster, more efficient web applications that delight users.

In Book 3, "Advanced AJAX Strategies: Scalable Solutions for Complex Web Applications," the focus shifts to advanced

AJAX strategies tailored for complex web applications. You'll learn how to tackle challenges such as managing concurrent requests, implementing server-side pagination, and integrating AJAX with backend technologies. With a focus on scalability and robustness, this book empowers developers to architect sophisticated solutions that meet the demands of modern web development.

Finally, Book 4, "Mastering AJAX: Architecting Robust Web and Mobile Solutions," offers a comprehensive overview of advanced AJAX topics. From real-time updates to security considerations and offline support, this book covers all aspects of AJAX development. By mastering these advanced techniques, developers will gain the expertise needed to architect robust web and mobile solutions that excel in today's digital landscape.

Whether you're a beginner looking to build dynamic web interfaces or an experienced developer seeking to master advanced AJAX strategies, this book bundle has something for everyone. With practical insights, real-world examples, and step-by-step tutorials, you'll be well-equipped to create powerful, responsive, and scalable applications that push the boundaries of web and mobile development. So, let's dive in and unlock the full potential of AJAX programming together!

BOOK 1
AJAX PROGRAMMING FOR BEGINNERS
BUILDING DYNAMIC WEB INTERFACES

ROB BOTWRIGHT

Chapter 1: Introduction to AJAX

AJAX Fundamentals delve into the core principles and techniques that underpin asynchronous JavaScript and XMLHttpRequest (XHR) interactions in web development. AJAX, short for Asynchronous JavaScript and XML, is a pivotal technology in modern web development, enabling dynamic and interactive user experiences without requiring full page reloads. It allows web applications to asynchronously exchange data with a server, updating parts of a web page without the need for a complete refresh. To harness the power of AJAX, developers must first grasp its fundamental concepts and best practices.

At the heart of AJAX lies asynchronous communication, a paradigm shift from traditional synchronous requests. Instead of waiting for a response before proceeding, asynchronous requests enable simultaneous operations, enhancing responsiveness and user experience. To initiate AJAX requests, developers utilize the XMLHttpRequest object, a JavaScript API that facilitates communication between the client and server. With XMLHttpRequest, developers can send HTTP requests to a server and handle server responses dynamically, enabling seamless data exchange.

One of the key components of AJAX is its ability to handle various data formats, with JSON (JavaScript

Object Notation) and XML (eXtensible Markup Language) being the most common. JSON has emerged as the preferred format due to its lightweight and human-readable structure, making it ideal for data interchange in AJAX applications. Developers can parse JSON data effortlessly in JavaScript, facilitating seamless integration with web applications. XML, although less prevalent in modern AJAX development, still offers flexibility for certain use cases.

To integrate AJAX functionality into web applications, developers leverage event-driven programming paradigms. Events such as button clicks or form submissions trigger AJAX requests, initiating dynamic updates to the web page content. By binding event listeners to DOM elements, developers can orchestrate AJAX interactions seamlessly, enhancing user interactivity. Moreover, event delegation techniques optimize event handling in AJAX-rich applications, ensuring efficient performance across various user interactions.

AJAX's versatility extends beyond simple data retrieval, encompassing complex operations such as form submission and validation. With AJAX, developers can submit form data asynchronously, validating user input in real-time without reloading the entire page. By intercepting form submissions with JavaScript event handlers, developers can prevent default browser behavior and execute custom AJAX requests, validating input fields against predefined criteria. This dynamic validation process enhances user experience by providing instant feedback on input errors.

As web applications grow in complexity, AJAX plays a crucial role in managing client-server interactions efficiently. AJAX pagination, for instance, enables seamless navigation through large datasets by fetching and displaying data subsets dynamically. By dividing content into manageable chunks, AJAX pagination optimizes performance and improves user experience, especially in content-heavy applications. Implementing AJAX pagination involves coordinating client-side requests with server-side logic to retrieve paginated data efficiently.

Cross-Origin Resource Sharing (CORS) is another fundamental aspect of AJAX development, essential for integrating resources from different origins securely. CORS allows web servers to specify which origins have permission to access their resources, mitigating potential security risks associated with cross-origin requests. Developers can configure CORS policies on the server side to specify allowed origins, methods, and headers, ensuring controlled access to resources across domains. By adhering to CORS best practices, developers can prevent unauthorized access and safeguard sensitive data in AJAX applications.

AJAX caching strategies are indispensable for optimizing performance and reducing server load in web applications. By caching AJAX responses locally, developers can minimize redundant requests and improve application responsiveness. Implementing client-side caching involves storing AJAX responses in the browser's cache, allowing subsequent requests for the same resource to be fulfilled locally. Additionally, developers can leverage HTTP caching headers to control caching behavior and specify cache expiration policies, ensuring data consistency and freshness.

To enhance the scalability and maintainability of AJAX applications, developers adopt architectural patterns and design principles tailored to asynchronous workflows. Model-View-Controller (MVC) architecture, for example, promotes separation of concerns, dividing application logic into distinct layers for improved modularity and code organization. By decoupling data, presentation, and business logic, MVC facilitates extensibility and scalability in AJAX applications, enabling seamless integration with evolving requirements and technologies.

In the realm of modern web development, AJAX continues to evolve alongside emerging trends and technologies, such as Progressive Web Apps (PWAs) and serverless architectures. Integrating AJAX with PWAs enables offline capabilities and seamless user experiences across devices, blurring the lines between web and native applications. Leveraging service workers and caching strategies, developers can enhance reliability and performance in PWAs, ensuring consistent access to critical resources regardless of network conditions.

Serverless architectures, characterized by event-driven, ephemeral compute services, present new opportunities for AJAX development, enabling scalable and cost-effective solutions. By leveraging serverless platforms such as AWS Lambda or Azure Functions, developers can offload backend tasks and focus on building responsive client-side experiences with AJAX. Integrating AJAX with serverless functions enables dynamic data processing and real-time interactions, empowering developers to deliver robust web applications with minimal infrastructure overhead.

In summary, mastering AJAX fundamentals is essential for building dynamic and responsive web applications that deliver exceptional user experiences. By understanding the core principles of asynchronous communication, data interchange formats, and event-driven programming, developers can unlock the full potential of AJAX in modern web development. From optimizing performance and scalability to ensuring security and compatibility, AJAX remains a cornerstone technology for crafting innovative and engaging web experiences.

Evolution of Web Development has been marked by significant advancements and shifts in technology, shaping the way websites and web applications are built and experienced. From the early days of static

HTML pages to the modern era of dynamic and interactive web applications, the journey of web development has been nothing short of transformative. It all began with the invention of HTML (Hypertext Markup Language), the standard markup language for creating web pages, which provided a simple way to structure and display content on the internet. As the internet gained popularity in the 1990s, web development evolved rapidly, with the introduction of technologies like CSS (Cascading Style Sheets) for styling web pages and JavaScript for adding interactivity to websites.

During the early stages of web development, websites were primarily static, consisting of simple HTML pages with minimal styling and functionality. However, as the demand for more dynamic and interactive web experiences grew, developers began exploring new techniques and technologies to meet these evolving expectations. This led to the emergence of server-side scripting languages like PHP, ASP, and JSP, which enabled developers to generate dynamic content on the server and deliver personalized experiences to users based on their interactions with the website. With server-side scripting, developers could create dynamic web applications that could retrieve and manipulate data from databases, handle user authentication, and perform various other tasks, all without requiring the user to reload the entire page.

As the capabilities of web browsers improved and broadband internet became more widespread, the focus of web development shifted towards client-side technologies, leading to the rise of AJAX (Asynchronous JavaScript and XML). AJAX revolutionized web development by enabling asynchronous communication between the client and server, allowing web pages to fetch data in the background and update specific parts of the page dynamically without needing to reload the entire page. This resulted in a more seamless and responsive user experience, paving the way for the development of single-page applications (SPAs) and other highly interactive web applications.

In parallel with advancements in client-side technologies, the rise of web frameworks and libraries played a significant role in shaping the modern landscape of web development. Frameworks like AngularJS, React, and Vue.js provided developers with powerful tools and abstractions for building complex web applications more efficiently, with features like component-based architecture, data binding, and virtual DOM rendering. These frameworks abstract away many of the low-level details of web development, allowing developers to focus more on building features and less on boilerplate code.

Moreover, the adoption of responsive web design principles became increasingly important as the usage of mobile devices for browsing the internet surged. Responsive web design aims to create web pages that adapt and display optimally across a wide range of devices and screen sizes, ensuring a consistent user experience regardless of the device being used. This approach involves using techniques like fluid grids, flexible images, and media queries to design websites that can seamlessly transition between desktops, laptops, tablets, and smartphones without sacrificing usability or functionality.

In recent years, the proliferation of web development tools and technologies has further accelerated the pace of innovation in the field. The advent of static site generators like Jekyll, Hugo, and Gatsby has made it easier for developers to create fast and efficient websites using modern web technologies like Markdown, React, and GraphQL, without the need for complex server-side setups. These tools enable developers to build websites as a collection of static files that can be deployed to content delivery networks (CDNs) for blazing-fast performance and global scalability.

Furthermore, the rise of serverless architecture has introduced a paradigm shift in how web applications are deployed and scaled. Serverless computing platforms like AWS Lambda, Google Cloud Functions, and Azure Functions allow developers to build and deploy applications without managing servers or infrastructure. Instead, developers can focus on writing code in the form of stateless functions that respond to events triggered by user interactions or external triggers. This serverless approach offers benefits such as automatic scaling, reduced operational overhead, and pay-as-you-go pricing, making it an attractive option for building highly scalable and cost-effective web applications.

In summary, the Evolution of Web Development has been characterized by continuous innovation and adaptation to meet the ever-changing demands of users and technology. From the early days of static HTML pages to the modern era of dynamic, responsive, and serverless web applications, the journey of web development has been shaped by advancements in HTML, CSS, JavaScript, server-side scripting, frameworks, responsive design, and serverless architecture. As technology continues to evolve, web developers must stay abreast of emerging trends and technologies to build fast, secure, and engaging web experiences that delight users and drive business success.

Chapter 2: Understanding Asynchronous JavaScript

Synchronous vs. Asynchronous Execution is a fundamental concept in computer science and programming, influencing how tasks are performed and managed within software applications. At its core, synchronous execution refers to the sequential execution of tasks, where each task must wait for the previous one to complete before it can begin. In contrast, asynchronous execution allows tasks to be executed concurrently, without blocking the execution of other tasks. This distinction is crucial for understanding various programming paradigms, especially in contexts where performance, responsiveness, and resource utilization are paramount.

In synchronous execution, tasks are executed one after the other in a predetermined order, with each task blocking the execution of subsequent tasks until it completes. This sequential nature of synchronous execution makes it easy to reason about the flow of control within a program, as tasks are executed in a predictable manner. However, synchronous execution can lead to performance bottlenecks, especially when dealing with tasks that are computationally intensive or involve waiting for external resources, such as network requests or file I/O operations. In such cases, the entire program may be delayed while waiting for a single task to complete, resulting in decreased responsiveness and efficiency.

To illustrate synchronous execution, consider a simple program that reads data from a file and performs some computation on it. In a synchronous implementation, the program would first open the file, read its contents, perform the computation, and then close the file. Each of these steps would be executed sequentially, with the program waiting for each step to complete before moving on to the next one. While this approach may be straightforward to implement and understand, it may not be the most efficient or scalable solution, especially if the file is large or the computation is time-consuming.

On the other hand, asynchronous execution allows tasks to be executed concurrently, enabling the program to continue executing other tasks while waiting for certain operations to complete. This concurrency is achieved by using non-blocking operations, where tasks are initiated and allowed to run in the background without waiting for their completion. As a result, the program can remain responsive and performant, even when dealing with tasks that may take a long time to complete.

One of the most common examples of asynchronous execution is asynchronous I/O, where input and output operations are performed asynchronously, allowing the program to continue executing other tasks while waiting for data to be read from or written to external sources. This approach is particularly useful in scenarios where the program needs to handle multiple I/O operations concurrently, such as serving multiple clients in a network server or processing large volumes of data from multiple sources.

In asynchronous programming, tasks are typically initiated using callbacks, promises, or async/await syntax, depending on the programming language and framework being used. Callbacks are functions that are passed as arguments to asynchronous functions and are invoked once the operation completes. Promises provide a cleaner and more structured way to handle asynchronous operations, allowing developers to chain multiple asynchronous operations together and handle errors more effectively. Async/await syntax, introduced in newer versions of many programming languages, offers a more intuitive and synchronous-looking way to write asynchronous code, making it easier to reason about and maintain.

To demonstrate asynchronous execution, let's revisit the example of reading data from a file and performing computation on it. In an asynchronous implementation, the program would initiate the file read operation and then continue executing other tasks while waiting for the read operation to complete. Once the read operation finishes, a callback or promise handler would be invoked to process the data and perform the computation. This approach allows the program to remain responsive and performant, even if the file read operation takes a significant amount of time.

In summary, understanding the differences between synchronous and asynchronous execution is essential for building efficient and responsive software applications. While synchronous execution offers simplicity and predictability, asynchronous execution provides concurrency and responsiveness, enabling programs to perform complex tasks efficiently. By leveraging asynchronous programming techniques and non-blocking I/O operations, developers can build applications that are more scalable, performant, and resilient to latency and resource constraints.

Callbacks and Promises are essential concepts in asynchronous programming, playing a crucial role in managing the flow of control and handling asynchronous operations in JavaScript and other programming languages. At their core, callbacks and promises provide mechanisms for executing code asynchronously, allowing developers to write non-blocking code that can handle tasks such as I/O operations, network requests, and event handling without blocking the execution of other code. Understanding how callbacks and promises work is fundamental for writing efficient, scalable, and maintainable asynchronous code in modern web development.

Callbacks are functions that are passed as arguments to other functions and are executed once a particular operation completes. In the context of asynchronous programming, callbacks are commonly used to handle the result of asynchronous operations, such as fetching data from a server or reading data from a file. When an asynchronous operation completes, the callback function is invoked with the result of the operation, allowing the program to continue executing other tasks while waiting for the asynchronous operation to finish.

To illustrate the use of callbacks, consider a simple example of fetching data from a server using JavaScript. In this example, we use the XMLHttpRequest object to send an HTTP request to a server and specify a callback function to handle the response once it is received. The code might look something like this:

```javascript
javascriptCopy code
// Define the callback function function handleResponse(response) { console.log('Response received:', response); } // Create a new XMLHttpRequest object var xhr = new XMLHttpRequest(); // Configure the request xhr.open('GET', 'https://api.example.com/data', true); // Set the callback function to handle the response xhr.onload = function() { if (xhr.status >= 200 && xhr.status < 300) { handleResponse(xhr.responseText); } else {
```

console.error('Request failed with status:', xhr.status); } }; // Send the request xhr.send();

In this example, the **handleResponse** function is defined as the callback function to handle the response from the server. When the XMLHttpRequest object receives a response from the server, it invokes the **onload** event handler, which in turn calls the **handleResponse** function with the response text. This allows the program to continue executing other tasks while waiting for the server response, ensuring a non-blocking and responsive user experience.

While callbacks are a powerful mechanism for handling asynchronous operations in JavaScript, they can lead to a phenomenon known as "callback hell" or "pyramid of doom" when dealing with multiple nested asynchronous operations. This occurs when callback functions are nested within each other, resulting in code that is difficult to read, understand, and maintain. To mitigate this issue, developers often use techniques such as modularization, named functions, and error handling to improve the readability and maintainability of callback-based code.

Promises provide a more structured and elegant way to handle asynchronous operations in JavaScript, offering better readability, error handling, and composability compared to traditional callback-based approaches. A promise represents the eventual completion or failure of an asynchronous operation and allows developers to chain multiple asynchronous operations together in a more concise and declarative manner. Promises have three states: pending, fulfilled, and rejected, and can transition between these states based on the outcome of the asynchronous operation.

To create a promise in JavaScript, you can use the Promise constructor, passing a function with two arguments: resolve and reject. Inside the function, you perform the asynchronous operation, calling the resolve function with the result if the operation succeeds, or the reject function with an error if the operation fails. For example:

javascriptCopy code

```
// Create a promise var fetchData = new Promise(function(resolve, reject) { // Simulate an asynchronous operation (e.g., fetching data from a server) setTimeout(function() { var data = { message: 'Data fetched successfully' }; // Resolve the promise with the fetched data resolve(data); }, 1000); }); // Handle the promise result fetchData.then(function(data) { console.log('Data:', data); }).catch(function(error) { console.error('Error:', error); });
```

In this example, we create a promise called **fetchData** that simulates fetching data from a server asynchronously using the setTimeout function. When the asynchronous operation completes successfully, the promise is resolved with the fetched data. We then use the **then** method to handle the resolved value (i.e., the fetched data) and the **catch** method to handle any errors that occur during the execution of the promise.

Promises offer several advantages over callbacks, including better error handling with the catch method, chaining multiple asynchronous operations together with the then method, and improved readability and maintainability of asynchronous code. Additionally, promises can be easily converted to async/await syntax, a newer and more intuitive way to write asynchronous code in JavaScript.

Async/await is a syntactic sugar built on top of promises that allows developers to write asynchronous code in a more synchronous-looking style, making it easier to read, write, and reason about asynchronous code. Async functions, marked with the async keyword, return promises implicitly and can contain await expressions, which pause the execution of the function until the promise is resolved. This allows developers to write asynchronous code that looks and behaves like synchronous code, without the need for callbacks or promise chaining.

To use async/await in JavaScript, you define an async function and use the await keyword to pause the execution of the function until a promise is resolved. For example:

```
javascriptCopy code
// Define an asynchronous function async function fetchData() { try { // Simulate an asynchronous operation (e.g., fetching data from a server) var data = await new Promise(function(resolve, reject) { setTimeout(function() { resolve({ message: 'Data fetched successfully' }); }, 1000); }); console.log('Data:', data); } catch (error) { console.error('Error:', error); } } // Call the asynchronous function fetchData();
```

In this example, the **fetchData** function is defined as an async function, allowing us to use the await keyword to pause the execution of the function until the promise returned by the inner Promise constructor is resolved. This allows us to write asynchronous code in a more synchronous-looking style, making it easier to understand and maintain.

In summary, callbacks and promises are fundamental concepts in asynchronous programming, enabling developers to write non-blocking code that can handle asynchronous operations efficiently and effectively. While callbacks provide a basic mechanism for handling asynchronous operations, promises offer a more structured and elegant way to handle asynchronous code, with better error handling and composability. Additionally, async/await syntax provides a more intuitive and synchronous-looking way to write asynchronous code, further improving the readability and maintainability of asynchronous JavaScript applications. Understanding how callbacks, promises, and async/await work is essential for building scalable, responsive, and maintainable web applications in modern web development.

Chapter 3: Working with XMLHTTPRequest

Creating XMLHTTPRequest objects is a fundamental aspect of web development, particularly when working with asynchronous JavaScript and XML (AJAX) to enable dynamic communication between a web browser and a server without requiring a page refresh. The XMLHttpRequest (XHR) object, introduced by Microsoft in the late 1990s and standardized by the World Wide Web Consortium (W3C), serves as the cornerstone for making HTTP requests from client-side JavaScript. To create an XMLHttpRequest object in JavaScript, developers typically use the **XMLHttpRequest()** constructor function, which returns a new instance of the XHR object.

In its simplest form, creating an XMLHttpRequest object involves invoking the constructor function without any arguments, as shown below:

javascriptCopy code

```
var xhr = new XMLHttpRequest();
```

This line of code creates a new instance of the XMLHttpRequest object and assigns it to the variable **xhr**. Once created, the XHR object can be used to make various types of HTTP requests, such as GET, POST, PUT, DELETE, and more, to interact with web servers and retrieve or send data asynchronously.

However, it's important to note that the XMLHttpRequest constructor is widely supported in modern web browsers, but it may not be available in older browsers, particularly Internet Explorer 6 and earlier versions. To ensure compatibility with older browsers, developers often use feature detection to determine whether the browser supports XMLHttpRequest and provide fallback mechanisms if necessary.

Once an XMLHttpRequest object is created, developers can configure and send HTTP requests using methods and properties provided by the XHR object. For example, to make a GET request to fetch data from a server, developers typically use the **open()** and **send()** methods of the XHR object:

javascriptCopy code

```
// Create a new XMLHttpRequest object var xhr = new XMLHttpRequest(); // Configure the request xhr.open('GET', 'https://api.example.com/data', true); // Send the request xhr.send();
```

In this example, the **open()** method is used to initialize the request by specifying the HTTP method (GET), the URL of the server endpoint (**https://api.example.com/data**), and whether the request should be asynchronous (**true**). Once the request is configured, the **send()** method is called to initiate the request and send it to the server.

Developers can also specify additional parameters and headers for the request using the

setRequestHeader() method of the XHR object. For example, to set a custom header such as **Authorization** for an HTTP request, developers can use the following code:

javascriptCopy code

```
xhr.setRequestHeader('Authorization',     'Bearer <access_token>');
```

This line of code sets the **Authorization** header of the request to include an access token, which is commonly used for authentication and authorization purposes when accessing protected resources on a server.

In addition to making GET requests, developers can use XMLHttpRequest objects to make other types of HTTP requests, such as POST requests for sending data to a server. To make a POST request, developers need to specify the request method as **POST** in the **open()** method and include the data to be sent in the body of the request using the **send()** method. For example:

javascriptCopy code

```
// Create a new XMLHttpRequest object var xhr = new XMLHttpRequest(); // Configure the request xhr.open('POST',     'https://api.example.com/data', true);   // Set  the  content  type  header xhr.setRequestHeader('Content-Type', 'application/json'); // Define the data to be sent var
```

data = JSON.stringify({ key: 'value' }); // Send the request with the data xhr.send(data);

In this example, the **open()** method is used to initialize a POST request to the server endpoint **https://api.example.com/data**, and the **setRequestHeader()** method is used to set the **Content-Type** header to **application/json** to indicate that the request body contains JSON data. The data to be sent is defined as a JSON string using the **JSON.stringify()** method, and it is sent with the request using the **send()** method.

In addition to making basic HTTP requests, XMLHttpRequest objects provide event handling mechanisms to monitor the progress and status of requests and handle the response from the server. Developers can register event listeners for various events such as **load**, **error**, **abort**, and **progress** to handle different aspects of the request lifecycle. For example, to handle the response from a server, developers can listen for the **load** event and define a callback function to process the response data:

javascriptCopy code

```
// Listen for the 'load' event
xhr.addEventListener('load', function() { // Check if the request was successful (status code 2xx) if (xhr.status >= 200 && xhr.status < 300) { // Parse the response JSON data var responseData = JSON.parse(xhr.responseText); // Handle the response data console.log('Response data:',
```

responseData); } else { // Handle HTTP errors console.error('Request failed with status:', xhr.status); } });

In this example, the **addEventListener()** method is used to register a callback function to handle the **load** event, which is triggered when the request completes successfully. Inside the callback function, the response data is parsed from JSON format using the **JSON.parse()** method, and it is then processed or displayed as needed.

Overall, creating XMLHttpRequest objects is a fundamental aspect of web development, enabling developers to make asynchronous HTTP requests from client-side JavaScript to interact with web servers and retrieve or send data dynamically. By understanding how to create and use XMLHttpRequest objects effectively, developers can build powerful and responsive web applications that provide a seamless user experience.

Making GET and POST requests is a fundamental aspect of web development, allowing developers to interact with web servers and exchange data between client-side JavaScript and server-side applications. GET and POST are two of the most commonly used HTTP methods, each serving distinct purposes in the context of web development. GET requests are typically used for retrieving data from a server, while POST requests are used for sending data to a server to be processed or stored. Understanding how to make GET and POST requests effectively is essential for building dynamic and interactive web applications that can fetch data from external APIs, submit form data, and interact with backend services.

To make a GET request in JavaScript, developers can use the XMLHttpRequest (XHR) object or fetch API, both of which provide mechanisms for making HTTP requests from client-side code. With the XHR object, developers can create an instance of the XMLHttpRequest object and configure it to make a GET request to a specified URL. The basic steps for making a GET request with XHR are as follows:

javascriptCopy code

```
// Create a new XMLHttpRequest object var xhr = new XMLHttpRequest(); // Configure the request xhr.open('GET', 'https://api.example.com/data', true); // Set up event listener to handle response xhr.onload = function() { if (xhr.status >= 200 && xhr.status < 300) { // Request was successful, handle response data console.log('Response:', xhr.responseText); } else { // Request failed, handle error console.error('Request failed with status:', xhr.status); } }; // Send the request xhr.send();
```

In this example, a new instance of the XMLHttpRequest object is created using the **new XMLHttpRequest()** constructor. The **open()** method is then called to configure the request, specifying the

HTTP method (GET), the URL of the server endpoint (**https://api.example.com/data**), and whether the request should be asynchronous (**true**). An event listener is set up to handle the response when it is received, and the **send()** method is called to initiate the request and send it to the server.

Alternatively, developers can use the fetch API, which provides a more modern and streamlined way to make HTTP requests in JavaScript. With fetch, developers can make GET requests with a simple function call, as shown below:

javascriptCopy code

```
fetch('https://api.example.com/data')
.then(response => { if (!response.ok) { throw new Error('Request failed with status:', response.status);
} // Handle response data  return response.json(); })
.then(data => { console.log('Response:', data); })
.catch(error => { console.error('Error:', error); });
```

In this example, the **fetch()** function is called with the URL of the server endpoint (**https://api.example.com/data**) as its argument. The fetch function returns a promise, which resolves to the response from the server. Developers can then use the **then()** method to handle the response, parsing it as JSON using the **json()** method and logging the response data to the console. The **catch()** method is used to handle any errors that occur during the request.

While GET requests are commonly used for retrieving data from a server, POST requests are used for sending data to a server to be processed or stored. POST requests are often used when submitting form data, uploading files, or performing actions that modify server state. To make a POST request in JavaScript, developers can use the XHR object or fetch API, similar to making a GET request.

With XHR, developers can create a POST request by configuring the XHR object to use the POST method and include the data to be sent in the request body. The basic steps for making a POST request with XHR are as follows:

javascriptCopy code

```
// Create a new XMLHttpRequest object var xhr = new XMLHttpRequest(); // Configure the request xhr.open('POST', 'https://api.example.com/submit', true); xhr.setRequestHeader('Content-Type', 'application/json'); // Set up event listener to handle response xhr.onload = function() { if (xhr.status >= 200 && xhr.status < 300) { // Request was successful, handle response data console.log('Response:', xhr.responseText); } else { // Request failed, handle error console.error('Request failed with status:', xhr.status); } }; // Define the data to be sent var data = JSON.stringify({ key: 'value' }); // Send the request with the data xhr.send(data);
```

In this example, the XHR object is configured to make a POST request to the server endpoint **https://api.example.com/submit** using the **open()** method, and the **setRequestHeader()** method is used to set the **Content-Type** header to **application/json** to indicate that the request body contains JSON data. The data to be sent is defined as a JSON string using the **JSON.stringify()** method, and it is sent with the request using the **send()** method.

Similarly, with the fetch API, developers can make a POST request by passing an options object with the HTTP method set to POST and the data to be sent included in the body of the request. Here's how to make a POST request with fetch

Chapter 4: Handling JSON Data

Introduction to JSON (JavaScript Object Notation) is essential for understanding modern web development and data interchange formats. JSON is a lightweight and widely used format for representing structured data, particularly in web applications where it serves as a common data interchange format between client-side JavaScript and server-side applications. Understanding the basics of JSON is crucial for web developers, as it enables them to work with data in a consistent and efficient manner across different platforms and programming languages. JSON is often used to transmit data between a web browser and a server in AJAX applications, as well as in configuration files, APIs, and other data exchange scenarios.

At its core, JSON is a text-based data format that is both human-readable and machine-parseable. It is based on two simple data structures: objects and arrays. Objects in JSON are enclosed in curly braces {}, while arrays are enclosed in square brackets []. Objects consist of key-value pairs, where each key is a string and each value can be a string, number, boolean, array, or another object. For example, here's a simple JSON object representing a person:

jsonCopy code

```
{ "name": "John Doe", "age": 30, "isEmployed":
true, "hobbies": ["reading", "running", "cooking"],
"address": { "city": "New York", "zipcode": "10001"
} }
```
In this example, the JSON object represents a person with properties such as name, age, isEmployed, hobbies, and address. The name and age properties are strings and a number, respectively, while isEmployed is a boolean value. The hobbies property is an array containing strings representing the person's hobbies, and the address property is another JSON object representing the person's address with nested properties for city and zipcode.

JSON's simplicity and versatility make it an ideal choice for transmitting and storing structured data in web applications. It is widely supported across different programming languages and platforms, making it easy to work with JSON data in various environments. In JavaScript, JSON is a first-class citizen, with built-in support for parsing and serializing JSON data using the **JSON.parse()** and **JSON.stringify()** methods, respectively. For example, to parse a JSON string into a JavaScript object, developers can use the **JSON.parse()** method:

javascriptCopy code
```
var jsonString = '{"name": "John Doe", "age": 30}';
var jsonObject = JSON.parse(jsonString);
console.log(jsonObject.name); // Output: John Doe
console.log(jsonObject.age); // Output: 30
```

In this example, the **JSON.parse()** method is used to parse the JSON string **jsonString** into a JavaScript object **jsonObject**, which can then be accessed and manipulated like any other JavaScript object.

Similarly, to serialize a JavaScript object into a JSON string, developers can use the **JSON.stringify()** method:

javascriptCopy code

```
var jsonObject = { name: 'John Doe', age: 30 }; var
jsonString = JSON.stringify(jsonObject);
console.log(jsonString); // Output: {"name":"John
Doe","age":30}
```

In this example, the **JSON.stringify()** method is used to serialize the JavaScript object **jsonObject** into a JSON string **jsonString**, which can then be transmitted over the network or stored in a file.

JSON's ubiquity extends beyond JavaScript, with support for parsing and serializing JSON data available in most modern programming languages and frameworks. In Python, for example, developers can use the **json** module to work with JSON data:

pythonCopy code

```
import json # Parse JSON string into Python
dictionary json_string = '{"name": "John Doe", "age":
30}' data = json.loads(json_string)
print(data['name']) # Output: John Doe
print(data['age']) # Output: 30 # Serialize Python
dictionary into JSON string data = {'name': 'John
```

Doe', 'age': 30} json_string = json.dumps(data) print(json_string) # Output: {"name": "John Doe", "age": 30}

In this Python example, the **json.loads()** function is used to parse a JSON string into a Python dictionary, and the **json.dumps()** function is used to serialize a Python dictionary into a JSON string.

Similarly, in Node.js, developers can use the **JSON.parse()** and **JSON.stringify()** methods to work with JSON data:

```javascript
javascriptCopy code
const jsonString = '{"name": "John Doe", "age": 30}';
const jsonObject = JSON.parse(jsonString);
console.log(jsonObject.name); // Output: John Doe
console.log(jsonObject.age); // Output: 30
const data = { name: 'John Doe', age: 30 };
const jsonString = JSON.stringify(data);
console.log(jsonString); // Output: {"name":"John Doe","age":30}
```

In this Node.js example, the **JSON.parse()** method is used to parse a JSON string into a JavaScript object, and the **JSON.stringify()** method is used to serialize a JavaScript object into a JSON string.

JSON's widespread adoption and ease of use make it a versatile tool for working with structured data in web development. Whether used for transmitting data between client and server, storing configuration settings, or exchanging data between different systems, JSON provides a simple and efficient solution for representing and manipulating structured data in modern web applications. As developers continue to build increasingly complex and data-driven web applications, a solid understanding of JSON will remain essential for effective communication and interoperability between different components and systems.

Parsing and stringifying JSON data are fundamental techniques in web development, enabling the manipulation and transmission of structured data between client and server applications. JSON, or JavaScript Object Notation, is a lightweight data interchange format commonly used for representing data in human-readable text format. The process of parsing JSON involves converting a JSON string into a JavaScript object, while stringifying JSON involves converting a JavaScript object into a JSON string. These techniques are essential for handling data in web applications, allowing developers to interact with APIs, store and retrieve data from databases, and exchange data between different parts of an application.

To parse JSON data in JavaScript, developers can use the built-in **JSON.parse()** method, which takes a JSON string as input and returns a JavaScript object. This method is commonly used when receiving JSON data from an external source, such as an API response or a file, and converting it into a format that can be easily manipulated and accessed in JavaScript code. For example:

javascriptCopy code

```
var jsonString = '{"name": "John", "age": 30, "city": "New York"}'; var jsonObject = JSON.parse(jsonString); console.log(jsonObject);
```

In this example, the **JSON.parse()** method is used to parse the JSON string **jsonString** into a JavaScript object **jsonObject**. The resulting object contains properties such as **name**, **age**, and **city**, which can be accessed using dot notation (**jsonObject.name**, **jsonObject.age**, etc.) or bracket notation (**jsonObject['name']**, **jsonObject['age']**, etc.).

Similarly, to stringify JavaScript objects into JSON format, developers can use the **JSON.stringify()** method, which takes a JavaScript object as input and returns a JSON string. This method is commonly used when sending data to an external server or storing data in a file in JSON format. For example:

javascriptCopy code

```
var jsonObject = { name: 'John', age: 30, city: 'New York' }; var jsonString = JSON.stringify(jsonObject); console.log(jsonString);
```

In this example, the **JSON.stringify()** method is used to stringify the JavaScript object **jsonObject** into a JSON string **jsonString**. The resulting string contains the JSON representation of the object, which can be transmitted over a network or stored in a file.

Parsing and stringifying JSON data are not limited to client-side JavaScript applications; they are also commonly used in server-side environments, such as Node.js, to handle data exchanged between the server and client. For example, in a Node.js application, developers can use the **fs** module to read JSON data from a file, parse it into a JavaScript object, manipulate the data as needed, and then stringify it back into JSON format for storage or transmission. Here's an example:

javascriptCopy code

```
const fs = require('fs'); // Read JSON data from a file const jsonString = fs.readFileSync('data.json', 'utf8'); // Parse JSON data into a JavaScript object const jsonObject = JSON.parse(jsonString); // Manipulate the data jsonObject.age += 1; // Stringify the updated object back into JSON format const updatedJsonString = JSON.stringify(jsonObject); // Write the updated JSON data back to the file fs.writeFileSync('data.json', updatedJsonString, 'utf8');
```

In this example, the **fs.readFileSync()** method is used to read JSON data from a file named **data.json**, and the **JSON.parse()** method is used to parse the JSON string into a JavaScript object. The data is then manipulated as needed (in this case, incrementing the **age** property), and the **JSON.stringify()** method is used to stringify the updated object back into JSON format. Finally, the **fs.writeFileSync()** method is used to write the updated JSON data back to the file.

When working with JSON data in web development, it's important to handle potential errors that may occur during parsing or stringifying operations. For example, if the input JSON string is invalid or malformed, the **JSON.parse()** method will throw a **SyntaxError**, and if the input JavaScript object contains circular references or unsupported data types, the **JSON.stringify()** method may produce unexpected results. Developers can use **try...catch** blocks to handle such errors gracefully and provide meaningful error messages to users or log them for debugging purposes.

In addition to parsing and stringifying JSON data in JavaScript, there are also various online tools and libraries available that can assist with these tasks. For example, online JSON validators can be used to validate the syntax and structure of JSON data, while libraries like **jsonlint** and **json5** provide additional functionality for parsing and manipulating JSON data in JavaScript applications.

Overall, parsing and stringifying JSON data are essential techniques in web development for handling structured data in JavaScript applications. Whether parsing JSON data received from an external source or stringifying JavaScript objects for transmission or storage, understanding how to effectively manipulate JSON data is crucial for building robust and interoperable web applications. By mastering these techniques, developers can seamlessly exchange data between client and server applications, enabling rich and dynamic user experiences on the web.

Chapter 5: DOM Manipulation with AJAX

Dynamic content manipulation is a core aspect of web development, enabling developers to create interactive and responsive web applications that can dynamically update content based on user interactions, data changes, or other events. This technique allows developers to modify the content of a web page dynamically, without requiring a full page reload, providing a smoother and more seamless user experience. Dynamic content manipulation is achieved using a combination of client-side scripting languages such as JavaScript, along with HTML and CSS, to manipulate the Document Object Model (DOM) of a web page in real-time.

One common use case for dynamic content manipulation is updating the content of a web page based on user input or actions. For example, developers can use JavaScript event handlers to listen for user interactions, such as clicks, keystrokes, or form submissions, and dynamically update the content of the page in response. This allows developers to create interactive elements such as dropdown menus, accordions, or tabs, where the content of the page changes dynamically based on the user's actions.

To manipulate dynamic content using JavaScript, developers can use various DOM manipulation techniques, such as selecting elements using CSS selectors, modifying element attributes and properties, and adding or removing elements from the DOM. For example, to toggle the visibility of an element based on a user click event, developers can use the **addEventListener()** method to attach a click event listener to the element, and then use the **classList.toggle()** method to toggle the visibility of the element by adding or removing a CSS class that controls its display property.

javascriptCopy code

```
// Select the element to toggle var element = document.getElementById('toggleElement'); // Attach a click event listener to the element element.addEventListener('click', function() { // Toggle the visibility of the element element.classList.toggle('hidden'); });
```

In this example, clicking on the element with the id **toggleElement** will toggle its visibility by adding or removing the CSS class **hidden**, which controls its display property in CSS.

Another common use case for dynamic content manipulation is fetching data from an external source, such as a web API, and updating the content of a web page with the retrieved data. This technique, known as Asynchronous JavaScript and XML (AJAX), allows developers to fetch data from a server in the background without requiring a full page reload, and then dynamically update the content of the page with the fetched data.

To fetch data from a server using AJAX, developers can use the XMLHttpRequest (XHR) object or the fetch API, both of which provide mechanisms for making HTTP requests from client-side JavaScript. For example, to fetch data from a JSON API and update the content of a web page with the retrieved data, developers can use the fetch API as follows:

javascriptCopy code

```
// Fetch data from the API
fetch('https://api.example.com/data')
.then(response => response.json()) .then(data => {
// Update the content of the page with the fetched data
document.getElementById('dataContainer').innerHTML = data.message; }) .catch(error => {
console.error('Error fetching data:', error); });
```

In this example, the fetch API is used to fetch data from the API endpoint **https://api.example.com/data**. The response from the server is then parsed as JSON using the **json()** method, and the resulting data is used to update the content of the page by setting the innerHTML property of an element with the id **dataContainer**.

Dynamic content manipulation is not limited to client-side JavaScript; it can also be achieved using server-side technologies such as PHP, Python, or Node.js. For example, developers can use server-side scripting languages to generate dynamic HTML content based on data retrieved from a database or other data source, and then serve the generated content to the client.

In addition to manipulating content dynamically based on user interactions or data changes, developers can also use dynamic content manipulation techniques to create animations and transitions that enhance the visual appeal and usability of a web page. For example, developers can use CSS transitions and animations to create smooth transitions between different states of an element, or use JavaScript libraries such as jQuery or GreenSock Animation Platform (GSAP) to create more complex animations and effects.

Overall, dynamic content manipulation is a powerful technique in web development for creating interactive, responsive, and visually appealing web applications. By leveraging client-side scripting languages such as JavaScript, along with HTML and CSS, developers can create web pages that dynamically update content based on user interactions, data changes, or other events, providing a richer and more engaging user experience. Whether updating content based on user input, fetching data from external sources, or creating animations and transitions, dynamic content manipulation is essential for building modern web applications that meet the evolving needs of users and businesses alike.

Handling form submissions with AJAX is a crucial aspect of web development, allowing developers to create dynamic and interactive web applications that can submit form data to a server asynchronously without requiring a full page reload. AJAX, or Asynchronous JavaScript and XML, enables developers to make HTTP requests from client-side JavaScript code, allowing for seamless form submission and validation processes. This technique enhances user experience by providing instant feedback to users, preventing page refreshes, and allowing for smoother interactions.

To handle form submissions with AJAX, developers typically use event listeners to capture form submission events, prevent the default form submission behavior, serialize the form data into a format suitable for transmission, and then use AJAX to send the data to a server endpoint. This process enables developers to process form submissions in the background, validate the input data, and update the web page with the server's response without interrupting the user's workflow.

One common use case for handling form submissions with AJAX is submitting user-generated content, such as comments, reviews, or messages, to a server without reloading the entire web page. This allows users to interact with the application seamlessly, without experiencing delays or interruptions caused by page refreshes.

To handle form submissions with AJAX, developers typically attach event listeners to form elements to capture the form submission event. When the form is submitted, the event listener intercepts the event, preventing the default form submission behavior using the **preventDefault()** method, and then serializes the form data into a format suitable for transmission.

For example, consider a simple HTML form with fields for name and email:

htmlCopy code

```html
<form id="myForm"> <label for="name">Name:</label> <input type="text" id="name" name="name"> <label for="email">Email:</label> <input type="email" id="email" name="email"> <button type="submit">Submit</button> </form>
```

To handle the form submission with AJAX, developers can use JavaScript to attach an event listener to the form element and intercept the form submission event.

javascriptCopy code

```javascript
document.getElementById('myForm').addEventListener('submit', function(event) { // Prevent the default form submission behavior event.preventDefault(); // Serialize the form data var formData = new FormData(this); // Send the form data to the server using AJAX var xhr = new
```

XMLHttpRequest(); xhr.open('POST', 'https://api.example.com/submit', true); xhr.onload = function() { if (xhr.status >= 200 && xhr.status < 300) { // Request was successful, handle response data console.log('Response:', xhr.responseText); } else { // Request failed, handle error console.error('Request failed with status:', xhr.status); } }; xhr.onerror = function() { // Request failed, handle error console.error('Request failed'); }; xhr.send(formData); });

In this example, an event listener is attached to the form element with the ID **myForm**, listening for the **submit** event. When the form is submitted, the event listener intercepts the event using **event.preventDefault()** to prevent the default form submission behavior. The form data is then serialized using the **FormData()** constructor, which creates a new **FormData** object containing key/value pairs representing the form fields and their values.

The form data is then sent to the server using an XMLHttpRequest object (**xhr**) configured to make a POST request to the server endpoint **https://api.example.com/submit**. The **onload** event handler is used to handle the response from the server, logging the response data to the console if the request is successful. The **onerror** event handler is used to handle any errors that occur during the request process, logging an error message to the console if the request fails.

Another common use case for handling form submissions with AJAX is implementing form validation on the client-side before submitting the form data to the server. Client-side form validation allows developers to provide instant feedback to users, helping them correct errors before submitting the form.

To implement client-side form validation with AJAX, developers can use JavaScript to validate the form input data before submitting the form. For example, consider a simple HTML form with fields for name, email, and password:

htmlCopy code

```
<form id="myForm"> <label for="name">Name:</label> <input type="text" id="name" name="name" required> <label for="email">Email:</label> <input type="email" id="email" name="email" required> <label for="password">Password:</label> <input type="password" id="password" name="password" required> <button type="submit">Submit</button> </form>
```

To implement client-side form validation with AJAX, developers can use JavaScript to attach an event listener to the form element and intercept the form submission event.

Chapter 6: Form Submission and Validation

Client-side form validation techniques play a crucial role in web development, ensuring that user input is accurate, complete, and formatted correctly before it is submitted to a server. These techniques empower developers to enhance the user experience by providing instant feedback to users, reducing the likelihood of errors, and improving the overall usability of web forms. By implementing client-side form validation, developers can minimize the need for server-side validation, reduce the burden on server resources, and create more responsive and interactive web applications.

One of the most common techniques for client-side form validation is using HTML5 form validation attributes and constraints. HTML5 introduced a set of built-in validation features that allow developers to specify validation rules directly within the HTML markup of a form. These attributes include **required**, **minlength**, **maxlength**, **pattern**, **type**, and more, enabling developers to enforce constraints such as required fields, minimum and maximum lengths, and specific input formats (e.g., email addresses, URLs, etc.). For example, to require a field and specify a minimum length of 5 characters, developers can use the **required** and **minlength** attributes:

htmlCopy code

```
<input type="text" id="username" name="username"
required minlength="5">
```
In this example, the **required** attribute ensures that
the field must be filled out, while the **minlength="5"**
attribute specifies that the input must be at least 5
characters long. If a user attempts to submit the form
without meeting these requirements, the browser will
display an error message indicating the validation
error.

Another technique for client-side form validation is
using JavaScript to validate form data
programmatically. While HTML5 form validation
attributes provide basic validation capabilities,
JavaScript allows for more advanced validation logic
and customization. Developers can use JavaScript
event handlers, such as **addEventListener()** or form
onsubmit, to intercept form submissions and perform
custom validation logic. For example, developers can
check if a field contains a valid email address,
password strength, or whether two fields match (e.g.,
password confirmation). Here's an example of
validating an email address using JavaScript:

javascriptCopy code

```
document.getElementById('email').addEventListene
r('input', function(event) { var email =
event.target.value; var emailRegex =
/^[^\s@]+@[^\s@]+\.[^\s@]+$/; var isValid =
emailRegex.test(email); if (!isValid) {
event.target.setCustomValidity('Invalid email
```

address'); } else {
event.target.setCustomValidity(''); } });

In this example, an event listener is attached to the email input field, listening for the **input** event. When the user types into the field, the event handler function is invoked, which retrieves the value of the email input and validates it against a regular expression pattern for a valid email address. If the email address is invalid, the **setCustomValidity()** method is called to set a custom validation message, informing the user of the error. Otherwise, if the email address is valid, an empty string is passed to **setCustomValidity()**, indicating that the field is valid.

Additionally, developers can leverage JavaScript libraries and frameworks to simplify and streamline client-side form validation. Libraries such as jQuery Validation, Parsley.js, and Validate.js provide pre-built validation rules, error messages, and validation methods, allowing developers to implement complex validation logic with minimal effort. These libraries offer features such as remote validation (validating input against server-side endpoints), custom validation rules, and internationalization support. For example, using jQuery Validation, developers can easily define validation rules and error messages using the **validate()** method:

javascriptCopy code

```
$('#myForm').validate({ rules: { email: { required:
true, email: true }, password: { required: true,
```

minlength: 8 } }, messages: { email: { required: 'Please enter your email address', email: 'Please enter a valid email address' }, password: { required: 'Please enter your password', minlength: 'Password must be at least 8 characters long' } } });

In this example, the **validate()** method is called on the form element with the ID **myForm**, specifying validation rules for the email and password fields. The **rules** object defines the validation rules, such as requiring an email address and specifying a minimum length for the password. The **messages** object defines custom error messages for each validation rule, which are displayed to the user when a validation error occurs.

Overall, client-side form validation techniques are essential for ensuring data integrity, improving user experience, and enhancing the overall usability of web forms. By combining HTML5 form validation attributes, custom JavaScript validation logic, and third-party validation libraries, developers can create robust and user-friendly web forms that guide users through the input process, minimize errors, and provide instant feedback on validation errors. By implementing effective client-side form validation, developers can create web applications that meet the highest standards of usability, accessibility, and user satisfaction.

AJAX (Asynchronous JavaScript and XML) integration

within React applications is a vital aspect of modern web development, enabling developers to create dynamic, interactive, and responsive user interfaces. React, a popular JavaScript library for building user interfaces, provides a robust framework for managing components, state, and data flow within applications. Integrating AJAX functionality into React applications allows developers to fetch data from external APIs, update the UI based on user interactions or data changes, and create seamless user experiences without full page reloads.

One common approach to integrating AJAX in React is by using the built-in **fetch()** API or libraries like Axios to make HTTP requests from within React components. The **fetch()** API is a modern replacement for XMLHttpRequest (XHR) and provides a simpler and more flexible interface for making network requests. With **fetch()**, developers can make GET, POST, PUT, DELETE, and other types of requests to fetch data from a server.

To use **fetch()** within a React component, developers typically call the **fetch()** function within a lifecycle method or a component event handler. For example, to fetch data from an external API when a component mounts, developers can use the **componentDidMount()** lifecycle method:

javascriptCopy code

import React, { Component } from 'react'; class MyComponent extends Component {

```
componentDidMount()                              {
fetch('https://api.example.com/data')
.then(response => response.json()).then(data => {
// Update component state with fetched data
this.setState({ data }); }) .catch(error => {
console.error('Error fetching data:', error); }); }
render() { // Render component UI } }
```

In this example, when the **MyComponent** mounts, the **componentDidMount()** method is invoked, triggering the **fetch()** request to the specified API endpoint. Once the data is fetched successfully, the component's state is updated with the retrieved data using **this.setState()**. This causes the component to re-render with the updated data, reflecting changes in the UI.

Another approach to integrating AJAX in React is by using third-party libraries like Axios, which provides additional features such as request cancellation, interceptors, and global error handling. Axios offers a more feature-rich and expressive API compared to **fetch()**, making it a popular choice for AJAX requests in React applications.

To use Axios in a React application, developers typically install the Axios package via npm or yarn and then import it into their components. For example, to fetch data from an API using Axios, developers can use the **axios.get()** method:

```
bashCopy code
npm install axios
```

```
javascriptCopy code
import React, { Component } from 'react'; import
axios from 'axios'; class MyComponent extends
Component { componentDidMount() {
axios.get('https://api.example.com/data')
.then(response => { // Handle successful response
const data = response.data; // Update component
state with fetched data this.setState({ data }); })
.catch(error => { // Handle error
console.error('Error fetching data:', error); }); }
render() { // Render component UI } }
```

In this example, the **axios.get()** method is used to
make a GET request to the specified API endpoint.
Once the data is fetched successfully, the
component's state is updated with the retrieved data,
triggering a re-render of the component with the
updated UI.

Additionally, developers can leverage React hooks,
specifically the **useEffect()** hook, to perform AJAX
requests in functional components. The **useEffect()**
hook allows developers to perform side effects in
functional components, such as fetching data,
subscribing to events, or updating the document title.

```
javascriptCopy code
import React, { useState, useEffect } from 'react';
import axios from 'axios'; function
MyFunctionalComponent() { const [data, setData] =
useState(null); useEffect(() => {
```

```
axios.get('https://api.example.com/data')
.then(response => { // Handle successful response
setData(response.data); }) .catch(error => { //
Handle error console.error('Error fetching data:',
error); }); }, []); return ( // Render component UI ); }
```

In this example, the **useEffect()** hook is used to fetch data from the API when the component mounts (due to the empty dependency array **[]**). Once the data is fetched successfully, the **data** state is updated with the retrieved data, triggering a re-render of the functional component.

When deploying React applications with AJAX functionality, developers need to ensure that CORS (Cross-Origin Resource Sharing) policies are properly configured on the server to allow requests from the React application's origin. Additionally, developers should handle loading states, errors, and data manipulation gracefully to provide a seamless user experience. By integrating AJAX functionality into React applications, developers can create dynamic, interactive, and data-driven user interfaces that meet the demands of modern web development.

Chapter 7: Implementing AJAX in Modern Frameworks

Integrating AJAX (Asynchronous JavaScript and XML) functionality into Angular applications is a crucial aspect of developing dynamic and interactive web applications. Angular, a popular front-end framework maintained by Google, provides powerful features for building single-page applications (SPAs) with rich user interfaces. With AJAX, developers can fetch data from servers, update the application state, and synchronize the UI with the latest data without requiring a full page reload.

One of the primary ways to perform AJAX requests in Angular is by using Angular's built-in HTTP client module, **HttpClient**. **HttpClient** provides a streamlined API for making HTTP requests and handling responses in Angular applications. To use **HttpClient**, developers must first import the **HttpClientModule** in their Angular module and inject the **HttpClient** service into their components or services.

typescriptCopy code

```
import { HttpClientModule, HttpClient } from '@angular/common/http'; import { Injectable } from '@angular/core'; @Injectable({ providedIn: 'root' }) export class MyDataService { constructor(private
```

```
http:   HttpClient)   {}   fetchData()   {   return
this.http.get('https://api.example.com/data'); } }
```
In this example, a service named **MyDataService** is created to encapsulate the logic for fetching data from an API. The **HttpClient** service is injected into the service's constructor, allowing the service to make HTTP requests using the **get()** method. The **fetchData()** method fetches data from the specified API endpoint (**https://api.example.com/data**) using the **get()** method and returns an observable of the HTTP response.

To consume the data fetched by the service in a component, developers can subscribe to the observable returned by the **fetchData()** method.

typescriptCopy code

```
import   {   Component,   OnInit   }   from
'@angular/core';   import { MyDataService } from
'./my-data.service';   @Component({   selector:   'app-
my-component',          templateUrl:          './my-
component.component.html',   styleUrls:   ['./my-
component.component.css']      })      export      class
MyComponent   implements   OnInit   {   data:   any;
constructor(private   dataService:   MyDataService)   {}
ngOnInit() { this.dataService.fetchData().subscribe(
(response) => { this.data = response; }, (error) => {
console.error('Error fetching data:', error); }); } }
```
In this component, the **fetchData()** method of the **MyDataService** service is called within the **ngOnInit()**

lifecycle hook to fetch data when the component initializes. The **subscribe()** method is used to subscribe to the observable returned by **fetchData()**, allowing the component to receive and process the HTTP response. The fetched data is then stored in the component's **data** property for use in the template.

Another approach to performing AJAX requests in Angular is by using the **HttpClient** module's **post()**, **put()**, **delete()**, and other methods to perform different types of HTTP requests. For example, to send a POST request with data to a server, developers can use the **post()** method:

typescriptCopy code

```
import { Injectable } from '@angular/core'; import { HttpClient } from '@angular/common/http'; @Injectable({ providedIn: 'root' }) export class MyDataService { constructor(private http: HttpClient) {} postData(data: any) { return this.http.post('https://api.example.com/post', data); }}
```

Similarly, developers can use the **put()** method to send PUT requests, the **delete()** method to send DELETE requests, and so on. The **HttpClient** module provides a consistent and intuitive API for performing various types of HTTP requests in Angular applications.

When deploying Angular applications with AJAX functionality, developers need to ensure that CORS (Cross-Origin Resource Sharing) policies are properly configured on the server to allow requests from the Angular application's origin. Additionally, developers should handle loading states, errors, and data manipulation gracefully to provide a seamless user experience. By integrating AJAX functionality into Angular applications, developers can create dynamic, interactive, and data-driven user interfaces that meet the demands of modern web development.

Chapter 8: Error Handling and Debugging Techniques

Handling AJAX errors is a critical aspect of web development, ensuring that applications gracefully manage unexpected situations and provide users with helpful feedback. When performing AJAX requests, errors can occur due to various reasons such as network issues, server-side errors, or incorrect request configurations. Handling these errors effectively is essential to maintain application reliability and user satisfaction.

One common approach to handling AJAX errors is by using error handling mechanisms provided by JavaScript's native XMLHttpRequest (XHR) object or modern APIs like Fetch or Axios. With XMLHttpRequest, developers can define event listeners to handle different stages of the request lifecycle, including errors. For example, to handle errors with XMLHttpRequest, developers can attach an event listener to the **onerror** event of the XMLHttpRequest object:

javascriptCopy code

```
var xhr = new XMLHttpRequest(); xhr.open('GET',
'https://api.example.com/data', true);
xhr.onreadystatechange = function() { if
(xhr.readyState === XMLHttpRequest.DONE) { if
(xhr.status === 200) { // Request was successful,
```

handle response console.log('Response:', xhr.responseText); } else { // Request failed, handle error console.error('Request failed with status:', xhr.status); } } }; xhr.onerror = function() { // Error occurred during request console.error('An error occurred during the request'); }; xhr.send();

In this example, an event listener is attached to the XMLHttpRequest object's **onerror** event to handle errors that occur during the request. If an error occurs, the **onerror** event handler is invoked, allowing developers to log the error or perform additional error-handling logic.

Similarly, with Fetch API, developers can use the **.catch()** method on the Promise returned by the **fetch()** function to handle errors:

javascriptCopy code

```
fetch('https://api.example.com/data')
.then(response => { if (!response.ok) { throw new Error('Network response was not ok'); } return response.json(); }) .then(data => { // Handle successful response console.log('Response:', data); }) .catch(error => { // Handle error console.error('Fetch error:', error); });
```

In this example, if the fetch request encounters an error (e.g., network error or server error), the **.catch()** method is called, allowing developers to handle the error appropriately.

Another approach to handling AJAX errors is by using libraries or frameworks that provide built-in error handling capabilities. For example, Axios, a popular HTTP client library, allows developers to define global error handlers and interceptors to handle errors consistently across an application:

javascriptCopy code

```
axios.get('https://api.example.com/data')
.then(response => { // Handle successful response
console.log('Response:', response.data); })
.catch(error => { // Handle error
console.error('Axios error:', error); });
```

In this example, the **.catch()** method is used to handle errors that occur during the request. Additionally, developers can define global error handlers and interceptors using Axios' built-in functionality to handle errors globally or perform common error-handling logic, such as logging errors or displaying error messages to users.

When handling AJAX errors, it's essential to provide users with informative error messages that help them understand what went wrong and how to resolve the issue. Error messages should be clear, concise, and user-friendly, avoiding technical jargon or sensitive information that could confuse or frustrate users.

In addition to logging errors for debugging purposes, developers can also implement fallback strategies or retry mechanisms to recover from transient errors automatically. For example, developers can configure

AJAX libraries to retry failed requests a certain number of times or implement exponential backoff strategies to gradually increase the time between retries.

When deploying applications that handle AJAX errors, developers should also consider monitoring and logging solutions to track errors in production environments effectively. By monitoring AJAX errors in real-time and analyzing error logs, developers can identify and address issues promptly, ensuring a smooth user experience and maintaining application reliability.

In summary, handling AJAX errors is a crucial aspect of web development that requires careful consideration and planning. By implementing robust error-handling mechanisms, providing informative error messages, and leveraging libraries or frameworks with built-in error handling capabilities, developers can create resilient and user-friendly web applications that handle errors gracefully and maintain high levels of reliability and user satisfaction.

Cross-Site Scripting (XSS) is a common security vulnerability in web applications that allows attackers to inject malicious scripts into web pages viewed by other users. These scripts can hijack user sessions, steal sensitive information, or perform actions on behalf of the user without their consent. Preventing XSS attacks is essential for protecting the integrity and security of web applications and ensuring the safety of user data.

One effective technique for preventing XSS attacks is input validation and sanitization. Input validation involves verifying and validating user input to ensure that it conforms to expected formats, lengths, and types before processing or displaying it. By validating user input on both the client and server sides, developers can mitigate the risk of XSS attacks by rejecting or sanitizing potentially malicious input before it is processed or rendered.

To implement input validation and sanitization in web applications, developers can use libraries, frameworks, or built-in language features to validate and sanitize user input effectively. For example, in JavaScript, developers can use regular expressions or built-in functions like **encodeURIComponent()** to sanitize user input before using it in dynamic content or HTML attributes:

javascriptCopy code

```
const userInput = '<script>alert("XSS attack")</script>'; const sanitizedInput = encodeURIComponent(userInput);
console.log('Sanitized input:', sanitizedInput);
```

In this example, the **encodeURIComponent()** function is used to encode the user input **'<script>alert("XSS attack")</script>'** before embedding it in HTML content or attributes. By encoding user input, special characters and HTML tags are converted into their respective URL-encoded representations, preventing them from being interpreted as HTML tags and scripts by the browser.

Another approach to preventing XSS attacks is Content Security Policy (CSP), a security feature that helps mitigate the risks of XSS by restricting the sources from which resources can be loaded and executed on a web page. CSP allows developers to define a policy that specifies which types of content are allowed to be loaded and executed on a web page, including scripts, stylesheets, images, and fonts.

To implement CSP in web applications, developers can add a **Content-Security-Policy** HTTP header to the server's response headers or include a **<meta>** tag with the **Content-Security-Policy** directive in the HTML **<head>** section of web pages. The CSP policy specifies the allowed sources for scripts, stylesheets, images, fonts, and other types of content, restricting the execution of potentially malicious scripts and resources.

htmlCopy code

```
<meta http-equiv="Content-Security-Policy" content="script-src 'self' https://apis.example.com; style-src 'self' https://fonts.googleapis.com;">
```

In this example, the CSP policy restricts the execution of JavaScript from external sources (**'self'**), allowing scripts to be loaded only from the same origin as the web page (**'self'**) and from the specified API endpoint (**https://apis.example.com**). Similarly, stylesheets are allowed to be loaded from the same origin and from the Google Fonts CDN (**https://fonts.googleapis.com**).

Additionally, developers can use CSP directives like **sandbox** and **unsafe-inline** to further restrict the execution of scripts and inline JavaScript in web pages. The **sandbox** directive creates a restricted execution environment for embedded content, while the **unsafe-inline** directive disables inline JavaScript, preventing XSS attacks that rely on injecting scripts directly into HTML attributes or event handlers.

htmlCopy code

```
<meta http-equiv="Content-Security-Policy" content="script-src 'self' 'unsafe-inline'; sandbox">
```

In this example, the CSP policy restricts the execution of inline JavaScript (**'unsafe-inline'**) and creates a sandboxed environment for embedded content, providing an additional layer of protection against XSS attacks.

When deploying web applications with CSP, developers should thoroughly test their CSP policies to ensure that they do not inadvertently block legitimate resources or functionalities. Additionally, developers should regularly review and update their CSP policies to adapt to changes in the application's requirements and to address emerging security threats.

In summary, preventing XSS attacks requires a multi-layered approach that combines input validation, sanitization, and Content Security Policy (CSP) to mitigate the risks of malicious script injection in web applications. By implementing robust security measures and following best practices for XSS prevention, developers can protect the integrity and security of their web applications and safeguard the sensitive information of users against exploitation by attackers.

Chapter 9: Security Best Practices in AJAX

Cross-Origin Resource Sharing (CORS) is a critical security mechanism implemented in web browsers to prevent unauthorized access to resources from different origins. CORS protects against Cross-Origin Resource Sharing (CORS) is a critical security mechanism implemented in web browsers to prevent unauthorized access to resources from different origins. CORS protects against Cross-Site Request Forgery (CSRF) and other types of attacks by enforcing strict policies that govern how web browsers should handle cross-origin requests. When a web application makes a cross-origin request, the browser enforces CORS policies by adding specific HTTP headers to the request and response to indicate whether the request is allowed based on the server's CORS configuration.

To understand CORS security, it's essential to grasp the concept of the same-origin policy, which is a fundamental security feature implemented in web browsers to restrict interactions between resources from different origins. The same-origin policy dictates that web browsers should only allow requests from the same origin (i.e., domain, protocol, and port) to access resources and execute scripts. However, there are legitimate scenarios where web applications need to make cross-origin requests to fetch data from APIs or embed resources from external sources. CORS provides a standardized mechanism for web servers to declare their cross-origin resource sharing policies and relax the same-origin policy selectively.

One of the key components of CORS security is the CORS preflight request, which is an additional HTTP request sent by the browser to the server before making a cross-origin request with certain HTTP methods or headers. The preflight request, also known as an OPTIONS request, includes information about the intended cross-origin request, such as the HTTP method, headers, and origin. The server responds to the preflight request with CORS headers that indicate whether the actual cross-origin request is allowed. If the server approves the cross-origin request, the browser proceeds with the actual request; otherwise, it blocks the request and prevents access to the requested resource.

To configure CORS policies on a web server, developers can specify CORS headers in the server's HTTP responses to indicate which origins are allowed to access the server's resources. The most commonly used CORS headers are **Access-Control-Allow-Origin**, **Access-Control-Allow-Methods**, **Access-Control-Allow-Headers**, and **Access-Control-Allow-Credentials**. These headers control the access permissions for cross-origin requests, specifying the allowed origins, HTTP methods, request headers, and whether credentials (e.g., cookies, HTTP authentication) can be included in cross-origin requests.

bashCopy code

Example of configuring CORS headers in an Express.js application npm install cors

javascriptCopy code

```
const express = require('express'); const cors = require('cors'); const app = express(); // Enable CORS for all routes app.use(cors()); // Enable CORS for specific origins app.use(cors({ origin: 'https://example.com' })); // Enable CORS with custom options app.use(cors({ origin: ['https://example.com', 'https://api.example.com'], methods: 'GET,POST,PUT,DELETE', allowedHeaders: 'Content-Type,Authorization', credentials: true })); // Start the Express server app.listen(3000, () => { console.log('Server is running on port 3000'); });
```

In this example, CORS middleware is added to an Express.js application using the **cors** package to enable CORS for all routes, specific origins, or with custom options. The **cors()** function sets the necessary CORS headers in the server's responses to allow cross-origin requests from the specified origins and with the specified HTTP methods, headers, and credentials.

When deploying web applications with CORS security, developers should carefully configure CORS policies to balance security and functionality. Overly permissive CORS policies may expose sensitive resources to unauthorized access, while overly restrictive policies may prevent legitimate cross-origin requests and disrupt application functionality. Additionally, developers should implement additional security measures, such as CSRF tokens and input validation, to complement CORS security and protect against other types of attacks.

Overall, CORS security is an essential aspect of web application security that helps mitigate the risks of cross-origin attacks and unauthorized access to resources. By understanding how CORS works and implementing proper CORS policies, developers can create secure and robust web applications that safely interact with resources from different origins while protecting user data and maintaining the integrity of the application.

Chapter 10: Building a Complete AJAX-Enabled Web Application

Structuring AJAX-enabled applications is crucial for maintaining code organization, scalability, and maintainability. Asynchronous JavaScript and XML (AJAX) technology have become integral components of modern web development, allowing developers to create dynamic and interactive user experiences without requiring full page reloads. However, as applications grow in complexity, it becomes essential to adopt effective structuring techniques to manage code complexity, facilitate collaboration among team members, and ensure the long-term viability of the codebase.

One commonly used approach to structuring AJAX-enabled applications is the Model-View-Controller (MVC) architecture, which divides the application into three interconnected components: the model, the view, and the controller. In the MVC architecture, the model represents the application's data and business logic, the view represents the presentation layer or user interface, and the controller acts as an intermediary between the model and the view, handling user input and updating the model accordingly.

bashCopy code

Example of creating a new Angular project using the Angular CLI ng new my-app

typescriptCopy code
// Example of implementing MVC architecture in an Angular application ng generate component my-component --skip-tests

In this example, a new Angular project is created using the Angular CLI, and a new component named **my-component** is generated to represent the view layer of the application. Angular's component-based architecture aligns well with the MVC pattern, allowing developers to encapsulate logic and UI components into reusable and modular building blocks.

Another popular approach to structuring AJAX-enabled applications is the Flux architecture, which emphasizes a unidirectional data flow and a centralized data store. In Flux architecture, actions are dispatched to trigger updates to the application state, and the state is managed by stores, which contain the application's data and business logic. Views subscribe to changes in the state and update accordingly, ensuring a consistent and predictable user interface.

bashCopy code
Example of installing Redux library for state management in a React application npm install redux react-redux

javascriptCopy code
// Example of implementing Flux architecture with Redux in a React application import { createStore }

from 'redux'; import { Provider } from 'react-redux'; import rootReducer from './reducers'; const store = createStore(rootReducer); ReactDOM.render(<Provider store={store}> <App /> </Provider>, document.getElementById('root'));

In this example, the Redux library is installed in a React application to manage the application's state using the Flux architecture. Redux provides a centralized store to hold the application state, reducers to specify how state changes in response to actions, and middleware to handle asynchronous actions, such as AJAX requests.

Additionally, structuring AJAX-enabled applications often involves organizing code into modules or components based on functionality or feature sets. Modularization helps break down large applications into smaller, more manageable pieces, making it easier to understand, maintain, and extend the codebase over time. By separating concerns and encapsulating related functionality into modules or components, developers can achieve better code organization, reusability, and testability.

bashCopy code

```
# Example of creating a new Vue.js component using the Vue CLI vue create my-app
```

vueCopy code

```
<!-- Example of structuring Vue.js application with components --> <template> <div> <Header />
<Sidebar /> <MainContent /> <Footer /> </div>
```

```
</template> <script> import Header from
'./components/Header.vue'; import Sidebar from
'./components/Sidebar.vue'; import MainContent
from './components/MainContent.vue'; import
Footer from './components/Footer.vue'; export
default { components: { Header, Sidebar,
MainContent, Footer } }; </script>
```

In this example, a new Vue.js project is created using the Vue CLI, and the application's structure is organized into components representing different parts of the user interface. Vue.js's component-based architecture allows developers to compose complex UI layouts by combining reusable components, promoting code reusability and maintainability.

When structuring AJAX-enabled applications, developers should also consider adopting design patterns and best practices that promote separation of concerns, code modularity, and reusability. Design patterns such as the Repository pattern, Dependency Injection, and Observer pattern can help streamline code organization and promote good software engineering practices.

Furthermore, incorporating build tools, task runners, and package managers into the development workflow can simplify the process of managing dependencies, bundling assets, and automating repetitive tasks. Tools like Webpack, Gulp, and npm enable developers to streamline development workflows, optimize performance, and maintain consistency across projects.

bashCopy code

```
# Example of installing Webpack for module bundling in a JavaScript project npm install webpack webpack-cli --save-dev
```

jsonCopy code

```
// Example of configuring Webpack in a webpack.config.js file module.exports = { entry: './src/index.js', output: { path: path.resolve(__dirname, 'dist'), filename: 'bundle.js' } };
```

In this example, Webpack is installed as a development dependency in a JavaScript project, and a basic configuration file (**webpack.config.js**) is created to specify entry and output points for bundling JavaScript modules. Webpack simplifies the process of bundling and optimizing code for production deployment, allowing developers to focus on writing clean and maintainable code.

In summary, structuring AJAX-enabled applications is essential for managing complexity, promoting code organization, and ensuring the long-term maintainability of web applications. By adopting architectural patterns such as MVC or Flux, organizing code into modules or components, and leveraging design patterns and best practices, developers can create scalable, maintainable, and robust AJAX-enabled applications that meet the demands of modern web development. Additionally, incorporating build tools, task runners, and package managers into the development workflow can streamline development processes and improve productivity.

Integrating AJAX with backend technologies is a fundamental aspect of modern web development, enabling dynamic and interactive web applications that communicate with servers asynchronously. AJAX (Asynchronous JavaScript and XML) allows web pages to make HTTP requests to the server and update content without requiring a full page reload. To integrate AJAX with backend technologies effectively, developers need to consider various factors such as choosing the right backend framework, implementing RESTful APIs, handling CORS (Cross-Origin Resource Sharing), and securing communication between the client and server.

One common approach to integrating AJAX with backend technologies is by using server-side frameworks or libraries that provide robust support for handling HTTP requests and generating dynamic responses. Popular backend frameworks like Express.js for Node.js, Django for Python, Laravel for PHP, and Spring Boot for Java offer built-in features and middleware for processing AJAX requests and serving data to client-side applications. These frameworks simplify the development of backend

APIs and provide tools for routing, request handling, data validation, authentication, and authorization.
bashCopy code
Example of setting up Express.js backend mkdir backend cd backend npm init -y npm install express touch index.js

javascriptCopy code

```
// index.js const express = require('express'); const app = express(); // Define routes app.get('/api/data', (req, res) => { // Process AJAX request and send response res.json({ message: 'Data from server' }); }); // Start the server const port = process.env.PORT || 3000; app.listen(port, () => { console.log(`Server is running on port ${port}`); });
```

In this example, an Express.js backend is set up to handle AJAX requests by defining a route (**/api/data**) that returns a JSON response with sample data. The server listens for incoming requests on port 3000, and the response is sent back to the client-side application.

Another critical aspect of integrating AJAX with backend technologies is designing and implementing RESTful APIs (Representational State Transfer) that follow best practices for structuring resources and handling CRUD (Create, Read, Update, Delete) operations. RESTful APIs provide a standardized approach for building scalable and interoperable web services, making it easier for client-side applications to interact with backend servers using AJAX.

bashCopy code

```
# Example of setting up Django backend pip install django djangorestframework django-admin startproject backend cd backend python manage.py startapp api
```

pythonCopy code

```
# api/views.py from django.http import JsonResponse def get_data(request): # Process AJAX request and return JSON response data = {'message': 'Data from server'} return JsonResponse(data)
```

pythonCopy code

```
# backend/urls.py from django.urls import path from api.views import get_data urlpatterns = [ path('api/data', get_data), ]
```

In this example, a Django backend is set up with a RESTful API endpoint (**/api/data**) that returns a JSON response with sample data. The view function **get_data()** processes the AJAX request and generates the response using Django's **JsonResponse** class.

Handling CORS (Cross-Origin Resource Sharing) is another crucial consideration when integrating AJAX with backend technologies, especially when the client-side application and the backend server are hosted on different domains. CORS is a security mechanism implemented in web browsers to prevent unauthorized cross-origin requests, and it requires servers to include specific HTTP headers to indicate which origins are allowed to access resources.

bashCopy code

```
# Example of configuring CORS in Express.js backend
npm install cors
```

javascriptCopy code

```
// index.js const express = require('express'); const cors = require('cors'); const app = express(); // Enable CORS app.use(cors()); // Define routes // ... // Start the server // ...
```

In this example, the **cors** middleware is added to the Express.js backend to enable CORS for all routes, allowing cross-origin requests from any origin. Developers can also configure CORS to allow specific origins, methods, headers, and credentials as needed.

Security is another critical aspect of integrating AJAX with backend technologies, as AJAX requests may transmit sensitive data between the client and server. To ensure the security of communication between the client-side application and the backend server, developers should implement encryption, authentication, and authorization mechanisms to protect against data breaches and unauthorized access. Techniques such as HTTPS (Hypertext Transfer Protocol Secure), JWT (JSON Web Tokens), OAuth, and session management help secure AJAX-enabled applications and prevent security vulnerabilities.

In summary, integrating AJAX with backend technologies is essential for building modern web applications with dynamic and interactive features. By choosing the right backend framework, designing RESTful APIs, handling CORS, and ensuring security, developers can create robust and scalable web applications that provide seamless user experiences and securely interact with backend servers.

BOOK 2
INTERMEDIATE AJAX TECHNIQUES
ENHANCING USER EXPERIENCE AND PERFORMANCE

ROB BOTWRIGHT

Chapter 1: Advanced JSON Manipulation

JSON Schema Validation is a powerful technique used in web development to ensure the correctness and integrity of JSON data exchanged between client-side and server-side applications. JSON Schema is a vocabulary that allows developers to define the structure, format, and constraints of JSON data using a schema specification written in JSON format. By validating JSON data against a JSON Schema, developers can enforce data validation rules, perform input validation, and ensure data consistency and compliance with application requirements.

To start using JSON Schema Validation in a web application, developers first need to define a JSON Schema that describes the expected structure and properties of the JSON data. JSON Schema uses a schema definition language to specify constraints such as data types, formats, required properties, minimum and maximum values, and regular expressions for string validation. Once the JSON Schema is defined, developers can use various tools and libraries to validate JSON data against the schema.

bashCopy code

Example of installing JSON Schema validator library
npm install ajv

javascriptCopy code

```javascript
// Example of defining a JSON Schema const schema
= { type: 'object', properties: { name: { type:
'string', minLength: 1 }, age: { type: 'number',
minimum: 18 }, email: { type: 'string', format:
'email' } }, required: ['name', 'age'] };
```

In this example, a JSON Schema is defined using the Ajv library for JSON Schema validation. The schema specifies that the JSON data should be an object with properties **name**, **age**, and **email**, where **name** is a non-empty string, **age** is a number greater than or equal to 18, and **email** is a string formatted as an email address. The **required** keyword specifies that the **name** and **age** properties are mandatory.

javascriptCopy code

```javascript
// Example of validating JSON data against a JSON
Schema const Ajv = require('ajv'); const ajv = new
Ajv(); const validate = ajv.compile(schema); const
data = { name: 'John Doe', age: 25, email:
'john@example.com' }; const isValid =
validate(data); if (!isValid) {
console.error('Validation errors:', validate.errors); }
else { console.log('Data is valid'); }
```

In this example, the JSON data **data** is validated against the JSON Schema **schema** using the **validate()** method provided by Ajv. If the data is valid according to the schema, the validation passes, and the message "Data is valid" is printed to the console.

Otherwise, if the data does not conform to the schema, validation errors are logged to the console.

JSON Schema Validation can be integrated into various parts of a web application, including client-side validation in web forms, server-side validation in API endpoints, and data validation in backend services and databases. By validating JSON data against a JSON Schema, developers can ensure data consistency and integrity, prevent injection attacks, and protect against malicious or malformed data.

javascriptCopy code

```
// Example of validating JSON data in an Express.js route handler const express = require('express'); const app = express(); app.post('/api/users', (req, res) => { const data = req.body; // Validate JSON data against JSON Schema const isValid = validate(data); if (!isValid) { return res.status(400).json({ errors: validate.errors }); } // Process valid data // ... });
```

In this example, an Express.js route handler for creating users receives JSON data in the request body. The data is validated against the JSON Schema using the **validate()** method provided by Ajv. If the data is not valid according to the schema, a 400 Bad Request response is sent back to the client with validation errors.

Deploying JSON Schema Validation in a web application involves integrating the JSON Schema validation library into the application codebase, defining JSON Schemas for data validation, and incorporating validation logic into client-side and server-side components. Additionally, developers should consider error handling, logging, and reporting mechanisms to handle validation errors gracefully and provide feedback to users or administrators when validation fails.

In summary, JSON Schema Validation is a valuable technique for ensuring the correctness and integrity of JSON data in web applications. By defining JSON Schemas that describe the structure and constraints of JSON data and validating data against these schemas, developers can enforce data validation rules, protect against security vulnerabilities, and maintain data consistency and compliance with application requirements. Integrating JSON Schema Validation into client-side and server-side components helps create robust and reliable web applications that handle data securely and efficiently.

Managing HTTP headers efficiently is a critical aspect of web development, as HTTP headers play a vital role in controlling various aspects of the communication between clients and servers. HTTP headers are metadata components of HTTP requests and responses that provide information about the request or response, such as the content type, content length, caching directives, authentication tokens, and session cookies. Efficient management of HTTP headers is essential for optimizing performance, enhancing security, ensuring compatibility, and complying with web standards and best practices.

To effectively manage HTTP headers in web applications, developers need to understand the different types of HTTP headers, their purposes, and how to set, modify, and interpret them correctly. HTTP headers are classified into several categories, including general headers, request headers, response headers, and entity headers. General headers apply to both requests and responses, while request headers provide additional information about the client's request, and response headers convey information about the server's response. Entity headers are related to the content of the message body, such as the content type and content length.

bashCopy code

```
# Example of inspecting HTTP headers using cURL curl -I https://example.com
```

In this example, the **-I** option is used with cURL to send a HEAD request to the specified URL (**https://example.com**) and display the headers of the response. By inspecting HTTP headers, developers can examine the metadata associated with the HTTP response, such as the status code, content type, content length, and caching directives.

httpCopy code

```
HTTP/1.1 200 OK Date: Sat, 01 Jan 2022 12:00:00 GMT Content-Type: text/html; charset=UTF-8
```

Content-Length: 12345 Cache-Control: max-age=3600, public

In this example, the HTTP response includes headers such as **Content-Type** (indicating that the content is HTML with UTF-8 encoding), **Content-Length** (specifying the size of the response body in bytes), and **Cache-Control** (setting caching directives to cache the response for 3600 seconds and allow public caching).

Efficient management of HTTP headers involves optimizing their usage to improve performance and reduce overhead. One common optimization technique is HTTP header compression, which reduces the size of HTTP headers transmitted over the network, thereby minimizing latency and bandwidth usage. HTTP header compression techniques such as gzip and brotli compress header data before transmission, resulting in smaller packet sizes and faster response times.

bashCopy code

Example of enabling gzip compression in Apache web server sudo a2enmod deflate sudo service apache2 restart

In this example, the **deflate** module is enabled in the Apache web server configuration to enable gzip compression for HTTP responses. After enabling gzip compression, the web server compresses response data, including HTTP headers, before sending it to the client, reducing network traffic and improving page load times.

Another aspect of efficient HTTP header management is ensuring security and compliance with web standards and best practices. HTTP headers play a crucial role in implementing security measures such as Content Security Policy (CSP), Cross-Origin Resource Sharing (CORS), Strict-Transport-Security (HSTS), and HTTP Public Key Pinning (HPKP). By properly configuring security-related headers, developers can mitigate security risks, protect against common web vulnerabilities, and enhance the overall security posture of web applications.

bashCopy code

```
# Example of configuring Content Security Policy (CSP) headers in nginx sudo nano /etc/nginx/nginx.conf
```

nginxCopy code

```
# Add CSP headers to nginx configuration add_header Content-Security-Policy "default-src 'self'; script-src 'self' https://example.com; style-src 'self' https://example.com";
```

In this example, the Content-Security-Policy (CSP) header is added to the nginx web server configuration to specify a policy that restricts the sources from which scripts and styles can be loaded. The CSP header helps prevent cross-site scripting (XSS) attacks by defining a whitelist of trusted origins for loading scripts and styles.

Efficient management of HTTP headers also involves handling cookies, authentication tokens, and session management securely and efficiently. HTTP headers such as **Set-Cookie**, **Authorization**, and **Cookie** are commonly used for managing user sessions, authentication, and stateful communication between clients and servers. By properly configuring these headers and implementing secure authentication and session management mechanisms, developers can protect against session hijacking, CSRF attacks, and other security threats.

bashCopy code

```
# Example of setting an HTTP cookie using JavaScript
document.cookie = "session_id=abc123; path=/; expires=Sat, 01 Jan 2023 00:00:00 GMT; secure; HttpOnly";
```

In this example, JavaScript code is used to set an HTTP cookie named **session_id** with the value **abc123**, set to expire on January 1, 2023, and marked as secure and HttpOnly. The **secure** attribute ensures that the cookie is only transmitted over secure HTTPS connections, while the **HttpOnly** attribute prevents client-side scripts from accessing the cookie, enhancing security against XSS attacks.

In summary, efficient management of HTTP headers is crucial for optimizing performance, enhancing security, and ensuring compatibility in web applications. By understanding the different types of HTTP headers, their purposes, and best practices for setting and interpreting them, developers can create robust and secure web applications that deliver a seamless user experience while complying with web standards and security requirements. Proper configuration of HTTP headers, including compression, security, and session management, helps mitigate security risks, improve performance, and enhance the overall reliability and scalability of web applications.

Chapter 2: Optimizing XMLHTTPRequest Usage

Handling concurrent requests is an essential aspect of modern web development, especially in applications that experience high traffic or perform resource-intensive operations. Concurrent requests occur when multiple clients send requests to a web server simultaneously, and effective handling of these requests is critical for optimizing performance, ensuring responsiveness, and maintaining scalability. Next, we'll explore various techniques, strategies, and best practices for managing concurrent requests efficiently in web applications.

One of the primary challenges in handling concurrent requests is ensuring that the web server can process multiple requests concurrently without overwhelming system resources or impacting the responsiveness of other clients. Asynchronous programming is a common approach used to address this challenge, allowing web servers to handle multiple requests concurrently by utilizing non-blocking I/O operations and event-driven architectures. Asynchronous programming enables the server to continue processing requests while waiting for I/O operations to complete, thereby maximizing CPU utilization and reducing idle time.

bashCopy code

```bash
# Example of running a Node.js server with
asynchronous request handling node server.js
```

In this example, a Node.js server is started with asynchronous request handling capabilities, allowing it to handle multiple requests concurrently without blocking the event loop. Node.js utilizes an event-driven, non-blocking architecture that enables efficient concurrency handling and scalability for web applications.

Concurrency control mechanisms are another essential aspect of handling concurrent requests, as they help prevent race conditions, resource contention, and other concurrency-related issues. Techniques such as locking, thread synchronization, and transaction isolation ensure that critical sections of code are executed atomically and consistently, even in the presence of concurrent access from multiple clients. By implementing concurrency control mechanisms, developers can maintain data integrity, avoid conflicts, and ensure predictable behavior in multi-user environments.

```bash
bashCopy code
# Example of deploying a Redis server for distributed
locking docker run --name redis-server -d redis
```

In this example, a Redis server is deployed using Docker to provide distributed locking capabilities for concurrency control. Redis is a popular in-memory data store that supports atomic operations and distributed locks, making it suitable for implementing concurrency control mechanisms in distributed systems.

Scalability patterns such as load balancing, horizontal scaling, and sharding are essential for handling concurrent requests in distributed and high-traffic environments. Load balancing distributes incoming requests across multiple server instances to evenly distribute the workload and prevent overloading individual servers. Horizontal scaling involves adding more server instances to the application infrastructure to increase capacity and handle growing traffic levels. Sharding partitions data across multiple servers based on a predefined key, enabling parallel processing and improving throughput for data-intensive workloads.

bashCopy code

Example of deploying a Kubernetes cluster for horizontal scaling kubectl create cluster my-cluster

In this example, a Kubernetes cluster is deployed to enable horizontal scaling of web server instances. Kubernetes is a container orchestration platform that automates the deployment, scaling, and management of containerized applications, making it easy to scale web servers horizontally to handle concurrent requests effectively.

Caching is another effective strategy for handling concurrent requests and improving performance by reducing the need for repeated computation or data retrieval. Caching stores frequently accessed data or computed results in memory or storage caches, allowing subsequent requests for the same data to be served quickly without executing expensive operations. Techniques such as in-memory caching, CDN caching, and database query caching help reduce latency and improve responsiveness for concurrent requests.

bashCopy code

Example of setting up caching with Redis in a Node.js application npm install redis

javascriptCopy code

```
// Example of caching database query results with Redis in Node.js const redis = require('redis'); const client = redis.createClient(); function getCachedData(key) { return new Promise((resolve, reject) => { client.get(key, (err, data) => { if (err) { reject(err); } else { resolve(data ? JSON.parse(data) : null); } }); }); } function cacheData(key, data, ttl) { client.set(key, JSON.stringify(data), 'EX', ttl); }
```

In this example, a Node.js application uses Redis as an in-memory cache to store and retrieve database query results efficiently. The **getCachedData()** function retrieves cached data from Redis, while the **cacheData()** function stores data in Redis with an expiration time (TTL) to ensure cache freshness.

Handling concurrent requests is a multifaceted aspect of web development that requires careful consideration of architectural design, programming techniques, and infrastructure configurations. By employing asynchronous programming, concurrency control mechanisms, scalability patterns, and caching strategies, developers can effectively manage concurrent requests, optimize performance, and ensure the responsiveness and scalability of web applications in diverse deployment environments.

Chapter 3: Implementing AJAX Pagination

Client-side pagination techniques are indispensable tools for managing large datasets in web applications, offering users a seamless browsing experience while reducing server load and optimizing performance. Pagination involves dividing a dataset into smaller, manageable chunks, typically displayed on separate pages, allowing users to navigate through the data incrementally. Next, we'll explore various client-side pagination techniques, including traditional pagination, infinite scrolling, and virtual scrolling, along with their implementation and best practices.

Traditional pagination is a common approach where data is divided into fixed-size pages, with navigation links provided to move between pages. When a user requests a specific page, the corresponding data is fetched from the server and displayed. This technique is straightforward to implement and provides predictable navigation, but it may result in slower load times, especially for large datasets, as each page requires a separate server request and page reload.

bashCopy code

Example of implementing traditional pagination in a web application npm install axios

javascriptCopy code

// Example of fetching paginated data from a server using Axios const axios = require('axios'); async

```javascript
function fetchData(pageNumber, pageSize) { try {
const response = await
axios.get(`/api/data?page=${pageNumber}&pageSiz
e=${pageSize}`); return response.data; } catch
(error) { console.error('Error fetching data:', error);
return []; } }
```

In this example, Axios is used to fetch paginated data from a server endpoint (**/api/data**), with parameters specifying the page number and page size. The fetched data can then be rendered in the user interface, with navigation links allowing users to move between pages.

Infinite scrolling, also known as endless scrolling, is an alternative pagination technique where data is loaded dynamically as the user scrolls down the page. Instead of dividing the dataset into discrete pages, new data is fetched and appended to the existing content as the user reaches the end of the page. This technique provides a seamless browsing experience, eliminating the need for explicit navigation between pages and allowing users to explore the dataset continuously.

```bash
bashCopy code
# Example of implementing infinite scrolling in a web
application npm install react-infinite-scroll-
component
```

```javascript
javascriptCopy code
// Example of implementing infinite scrolling with
React import React, { useState, useEffect } from
```

```
'react'; import axios from 'axios'; import
InfiniteScroll from 'react-infinite-scroll-component';
const App = () => { const [data, setData] =
useState([]); const [page, setPage] = useState(1);
const fetchData = async () => { try { const response
= await axios.get(`/api/data?page=${page}`);
setData(prevData => [...prevData, ...response.data]);
setPage(prevPage => prevPage + 1); } catch (error) {
console.error('Error fetching data:', error); } };
useEffect(() => { fetchData(); }, []); return ( <div>
<InfiniteScroll             dataLength={data.length}
next={fetchData}                    hasMore={true}
loader={<h4>Loading...</h4>} > {data.map(item => (
<div       key={item.id}>{item.name}</div>        ))}
</InfiniteScroll> </div> ); }; export default App;
```

In this example, an infinite scrolling component from
the **react-infinite-scroll-component** library is used to
implement infinite scrolling in a React application. As
the user scrolls down the page, the **fetchData**
function is called to fetch additional data from the
server and append it to the existing content.

Virtual scrolling, also known as windowing or lazy
loading, is a performance optimization technique
where only a subset of the dataset is loaded into the
DOM at a time, based on the visible portion of the
viewport. As the user scrolls through the content,
new data is fetched and rendered dynamically, while

offscreen data is removed from the DOM to conserve memory and improve performance.

bashCopy code

Example of implementing virtual scrolling in a web application npm install react-window

javascriptCopy code

```javascript
// Example of implementing virtual scrolling with React Window import React, { useState } from 'react'; import { FixedSizeList } from 'react-window'; import axios from 'axios'; const App = () => { const [data, setData] = useState([]); const fetchData = async (startIndex, stopIndex) => { try { const response = await axios.get(`/api/data?startIndex=${startIndex}&stopIndex=${stopIndex}`); return response.data; } catch (error) { console.error('Error fetching data:', error); return []; } }; const Row = ({ index, style }) => ( <div style={style}>{data[index].name}</div> ); return ( <div> <FixedSizeList height={400} itemCount={data.length} itemSize={50} width={300} > {Row} </FixedSizeList> </div> ); }; export default App;
```

In this example, the **react-window** library is used to implement virtual scrolling in a React application. The **FixedSizeList** component renders only the visible portion of the dataset, recycling DOM elements as the user scrolls through the content.

Each pagination technique has its advantages and limitations, and the choice depends on factors such as the nature of the dataset, user experience requirements, and performance considerations. Traditional pagination provides predictable navigation but may result in slower load times for large datasets. Infinite scrolling offers a seamless browsing experience but requires careful management to prevent excessive server requests and memory consumption. Virtual scrolling optimizes performance by rendering only the visible portion of the dataset but may be more complex to implement.

By understanding the characteristics of each pagination technique and their implications for user experience and performance, developers can choose the most suitable approach for their specific use case and effectively manage large datasets in web applications.

Server-side pagination strategies are essential components of web application development, particularly when dealing with large datasets that need to be efficiently managed and presented to users. Unlike client-side pagination, where the entire dataset is retrieved and paginated on the client side, server-side pagination involves fetching only a subset of data from the server, based on the user's request. Next, we will delve into various server-side pagination strategies, their implementation techniques, and best practices to optimize performance and enhance user experience.

One of the most common server-side pagination techniques is the use of SQL queries with LIMIT and OFFSET clauses to retrieve a specific subset of data from a database. The LIMIT clause restricts the number of rows returned by a query, while the OFFSET clause specifies the starting point from which to retrieve rows. By combining these clauses with appropriate pagination parameters, such as page number and page size, developers can efficiently paginate through large datasets without overloading the server or consuming excessive resources.

bashCopy code

```
# Example of implementing server-side pagination
with SQL queries SELECT * FROM products LIMIT 10
OFFSET 0;
```

In this example, a SQL query is used to retrieve the first 10 rows from the "products" table, starting from the beginning of the dataset. Adjusting the OFFSET value allows fetching subsequent pages of data, while the LIMIT value determines the number of rows per page.

Another server-side pagination strategy involves leveraging frameworks or libraries that provide built-in pagination support, such as Spring Data in Java or Django ORM in Python. These frameworks offer abstractions and utilities for paginating query results, allowing developers to paginate through database records with minimal boilerplate code.

```bash
# Example of implementing server-side pagination
with Spring Data in Java Page<Product> products =
productRepository.findAll(PageRequest.of(pageNumber, pageSize));
```

In this example, Spring Data's **findAll()** method is used to retrieve a page of product entities from the database, with pagination parameters specified using the **PageRequest** class.

Pagination can also be implemented manually by writing custom logic to calculate the appropriate query parameters based on the user's pagination preferences. This approach offers more flexibility and control over the pagination process, allowing developers to tailor pagination behavior to specific requirements or performance considerations.

```bash
# Example of implementing custom server-side
pagination logic in Node.js const getPaginatedData =
async (pageNumber, pageSize) => { const offset =
(pageNumber - 1) * pageSize; const limit = pageSize;
const data = await fetchDataFromDatabase(offset,
limit); return data; };
```

In this example, a custom function **getPaginatedData** is defined to calculate the offset and limit values based on the requested page number and page size, before fetching the corresponding subset of data from the database.

Server-side pagination offers several advantages over client-side pagination, particularly in scenarios involving large datasets or security-sensitive information. By paginating data on the server side, developers can reduce network latency and bandwidth usage, improve scalability by offloading processing to the server, and ensure data privacy and security by controlling access to sensitive information. However, server-side pagination also has its challenges, such as increased server load and potential performance bottlenecks, especially when dealing with complex queries or large datasets. To mitigate these challenges, developers can employ various optimization techniques, such as indexing database columns, caching frequently accessed data, and optimizing query execution plans.

Additionally, server-side pagination should be complemented with efficient client-side pagination controls, such as pagination links or controls, to provide users with intuitive navigation and a seamless browsing experience. These controls allow users to navigate through paginated data easily and specify their pagination preferences, such as the number of items per page or the ability to jump to a specific page.

In summary, server-side pagination is a powerful technique for efficiently managing large datasets in web applications, offering benefits such as improved performance, scalability, and data security. By leveraging SQL queries, framework utilities, or custom pagination logic, developers can implement server-side pagination effectively and provide users with a seamless and responsive browsing experience, even when dealing with extensive datasets.

Chapter 4: Real-time Data Updates with AJAX

AJAX long polling is a technique used in web development to achieve real-time updates and notifications in web applications without the need for constant client-server communication. Unlike traditional AJAX requests, where the client sends a request to the server and waits for a response, long polling involves keeping an HTTP request open for an extended period, waiting for the server to send a response when new data is available. This approach enables servers to push updates to clients immediately as they occur, providing a near-real-time user experience. Implementing AJAX long polling involves configuring both the client and server sides to establish and maintain long-lived connections and handle data updates efficiently.

bashCopy code

```
# Example of implementing AJAX long polling in JavaScript const longPoll = () => { fetch('/api/updates') .then(response => response.json()) .then(data => { // Process data or trigger UI updates console.log('Received data:', data); // Start long polling again longPoll(); }) .catch(error => { console.error('Error occurred:', error); // Retry long polling after a delay setTimeout(longPoll, 5000); }); }; // Start long polling longPoll();
```

In this JavaScript example, the client-side code initiates a long polling request to the server by repeatedly sending AJAX requests to a specific endpoint (**/api/updates**). When the server has new data available, it sends a response back to the client, which processes the data or triggers UI updates accordingly. Subsequently, the client initiates another long polling request to listen for further updates. In case of errors or timeouts, the client retries the long polling process after a brief delay to maintain the connection with the server. On the server side, implementing AJAX long polling typically involves configuring the server to handle long-lived HTTP connections and manage the flow of data updates to connected clients. Depending on the server-side technology stack used, such as Node.js, Python with Django or Flask, or Java with Spring, the implementation may vary. However, the core concept remains consistent: keep HTTP connections open for an extended period and send responses when new data becomes available.

javascriptCopy code

```
// Example of implementing long polling with Express.js
in Node.js const express = require('express'); const
app = express(); app.get('/api/updates', (req, res) => {
// Simulate data updates every 5 seconds
setTimeout(() => { const data = { message: 'New data
available' }; res.json(data); }, 5000); });
app.listen(3000, () => { console.log('Server is running
on port 3000'); });
```

In this Node.js example using Express.js, the server responds to requests to the **/api/updates** endpoint by simulating data updates every 5 seconds. When new data is available, the server sends a JSON response containing the updated data to connected clients. This approach effectively implements long polling by maintaining long-lived HTTP connections with clients and pushing updates as they occur.

While AJAX long polling provides real-time updates and notifications in web applications, it has certain limitations and considerations. One major drawback is the potential for increased server load and resource consumption, as each open connection consumes server resources. Additionally, long polling may introduce latency and delays in delivering updates, especially in high-traffic or resource-constrained environments. Furthermore, long-lived connections can be susceptible to network timeouts, leading to connection drops and reconnections, which need to be handled gracefully on both the client and server sides.

To mitigate these limitations, developers can explore alternative real-time communication techniques, such as WebSockets or Server-Sent Events (SSE), which offer more efficient and reliable ways to achieve real-time updates in web applications. WebSockets, in particular, provide full-duplex communication channels between clients and servers, enabling bi-directional data transfer with low latency and minimal overhead. SSE, on the other hand, allows servers to push updates to clients over a single HTTP connection, offering a lightweight and standardized mechanism for server-to-client communication.

In summary, AJAX long polling is a viable technique for achieving real-time updates and notifications in web applications, albeit with certain limitations and considerations. By configuring long-lived HTTP connections between clients and servers and handling data updates efficiently, developers can implement long polling to deliver near-real-time user experiences in web applications. However, it's essential to weigh the trade-offs and explore alternative real-time communication methods, such as WebSockets or SSE, depending on the specific requirements and constraints of the application. WebSockets and AJAX are two popular technologies used in web development for achieving real-time updates and enabling interactive communication between clients and servers. While both serve the purpose of facilitating real-time interactions, they differ significantly in their underlying mechanisms, performance characteristics, and use cases. Next, we'll explore the differences between WebSockets and AJAX for real-time updates, including their features, implementation details, and considerations for choosing between them.

AJAX (Asynchronous JavaScript and XML) is a technique used to make asynchronous HTTP requests from the client to the server, typically to fetch data or perform actions without reloading the entire web page. AJAX requests are initiated by the client using JavaScript and are handled by the server, which processes the request and returns a response asynchronously. AJAX is well-suited for scenarios where periodic updates or data retrieval is required, such as fetching new messages in a chat application or refreshing dynamic content on a web page.

bashCopy code

```
# Example of making an AJAX request with jQuery
$.ajax({ url: '/api/data', method: 'GET', success: function(response) { console.log('Data received:', response); }, error: function(error) { console.error('Error fetching data:', error); } });
```

In this jQuery example, an AJAX request is made to the **/api/data** endpoint using the **$.ajax()** function. Upon successful completion of the request, the received data is logged to the console, while any errors are handled in the error callback.

WebSockets, on the other hand, provide a full-duplex communication channel over a single TCP connection, allowing bidirectional communication between clients and servers in real time. Unlike AJAX, which relies on traditional HTTP requests and responses, WebSockets establish a persistent connection between the client and server, enabling low-latency, high-performance communication. WebSockets are particularly suitable for applications requiring instant updates, such as real-time collaboration tools, multiplayer games, and financial trading platforms.

bashCopy code

```
# Example of setting up a WebSocket server with Node.js npm install ws
```

javascriptCopy code

```
// Example of implementing a WebSocket server in
Node.js const WebSocket = require('ws'); const wss
= new WebSocket.Server({ port: 8080 });
wss.on('connection', ws => { console.log('Client
connected'); ws.on('message', message => {
console.log('Received message:', message); // Process
message and send response ws.send('Response from
server'); }); ws.on('close', () => { console.log('Client
disconnected'); }); });
```

In this Node.js example using the **ws** library, a WebSocket server is created to listen for incoming connections on port 8080. When a client connects, the server logs the event and sets up event listeners to handle incoming messages and client disconnections. Upon receiving a message from the client, the server processes it and sends a response back to the client.

Comparing AJAX and WebSockets, AJAX is suitable for scenarios where periodic data updates are needed, and the overhead of establishing and maintaining persistent connections is not warranted. It is well-supported across all modern web browsers and is relatively straightforward to implement using JavaScript frameworks or libraries. However, AJAX requests are limited by the request-response model of HTTP, which may introduce latency and overhead, especially for frequent updates or real-time interactions.

On the other hand, WebSockets offer low-latency, bidirectional communication with minimal overhead, making them ideal for applications requiring instant updates and interactive features. WebSockets eliminate the need for repeated HTTP requests, reducing network latency and server load, and enabling real-time collaboration and synchronization between clients and servers. However, WebSockets require support from both the client and server, and additional considerations for handling connection errors and managing resources efficiently.

When choosing between WebSockets and AJAX for real-time updates, developers should consider the specific requirements and constraints of their application, such as performance, scalability, and compatibility with existing infrastructure. AJAX may be sufficient for applications with occasional updates or asynchronous interactions, while WebSockets offer superior performance and responsiveness for real-time communication and collaboration. Additionally, hybrid approaches combining both technologies, such as long polling with AJAX fallback, can provide a balance between real-time updates and compatibility with legacy systems or environments.

Chapter 5: Cross-Origin Resource Sharing (CORS) Implementation

CORS (Cross-Origin Resource Sharing) Preflight Requests are an essential aspect of modern web development, facilitating secure communication between clients and servers across different origins. Understanding CORS Preflight Requests is crucial for developers to ensure seamless interaction between web applications and resources from diverse origins while maintaining security standards. When a web browser detects a cross-origin request, it initiates an HTTP OPTIONS request to the server, serving as a preflight check to determine whether the subsequent cross-origin request should be allowed. This preflight request contains additional headers, such as Origin and Access-Control-Request-Method, providing essential information about the request's origin and intended HTTP method.

bashCopy code

```
# Example of handling CORS Preflight Requests in
Node.js with Express.js npm install cors
```

javascriptCopy code

```
// Example of enabling CORS in an Express.js server
const express = require('express'); const cors =
require('cors'); const app = express();
```

```
app.use(cors());   // Define routes and other
```
middleware

In this Node.js example using Express.js and the cors middleware, CORS is enabled globally for all routes by invoking the **app.use(cors())** method. This middleware automatically includes the necessary CORS headers in responses, such as **Access-Control-Allow-Origin: ***, permitting requests from any origin. Furthermore, developers can configure more granular CORS policies by passing options to the cors middleware, specifying allowed origins, methods, and headers. Effective handling of CORS Preflight Requests is crucial for ensuring the security and interoperability of web applications. These preflight requests prevent unauthorized cross-origin requests from accessing sensitive resources, significantly reducing the risk of security breaches.

However, configuring CORS policies can sometimes pose challenges, particularly when dealing with complex web application architectures or integrating with external services. Developers must carefully assess their application's requirements and implement suitable CORS policies to strike a balance between security and usability. Alongside configuring CORS policies on the server side, implementing robust client-side security measures is also essential to mitigate potential risks associated with cross-origin requests.

For instance, developers can employ various techniques such as validating and sanitizing user input, utilizing secure authentication mechanisms like OAuth, and enforcing stringent Content Security Policies (CSP) to prevent unauthorized access to sensitive resources. By adopting a comprehensive approach to security, developers can minimize the likelihood of CORS-related vulnerabilities and ensure the integrity and confidentiality of their web applications. Despite the security benefits offered by CORS Preflight Requests, they may introduce additional complexity and overhead, particularly in scenarios involving intricate web application architectures or distributed systems.

Developers need to carefully evaluate trade-offs and consider alternative approaches, such as JSON Web Tokens (JWT) or proxy servers, to facilitate cross-origin communication without compromising security. In summary, CORS Preflight Requests play a pivotal role in web security and interoperability, allowing servers to enforce access control policies and prevent unauthorized cross-origin requests effectively. By understanding the mechanics of CORS Preflight Requests and implementing appropriate CORS policies, developers can ensure the security and reliability of their web applications while enabling seamless communication between clients and servers.

Chapter 6: AJAX Caching Strategies

Client-side caching techniques are integral components of modern web development, allowing for efficient storage and retrieval of resources on the client side to enhance performance and user experience. These techniques involve storing copies of resources such as HTML, CSS, JavaScript, images, and other assets in the client's browser cache, reducing the need for repeated requests to the server and minimizing network latency. Implementing client-side caching techniques can significantly improve page load times, decrease server load, and conserve bandwidth. Developers employ various strategies to leverage client-side caching effectively, including setting appropriate cache-control headers, utilizing browser caching mechanisms, implementing service workers, and employing local storage and session storage mechanisms.

bashCopy code
Example of setting cache-control headers in Node.js with Express.js npm install express

javascriptCopy code
// Example of setting cache-control headers in an Express.js server const express = require('express'); const app = express(); // Set cache-control header to instruct clients to cache responses for a specific

```
duration    app.use((req,    res,    next)    =>    {
res.setHeader('Cache-Control',    'public,    max-
age=3600'); // Cache responses for 1 hour  next(); });
// Define routes and other middleware
```

In this Node.js example using Express.js, cache-control headers are set to instruct clients to cache responses for a specified duration. The **max-age** directive indicates the maximum time in seconds that the response can be cached by the client. By setting appropriate cache-control headers, developers can control how browsers cache resources, balancing between caching efficiency and freshness of content.

Another effective client-side caching technique is leveraging browser caching mechanisms. Browsers automatically cache resources based on cache-control headers provided by the server. By setting longer cache durations for static assets such as images, stylesheets, and scripts, developers can ensure that these resources are cached by the browser for subsequent requests, reducing the need for re-downloading them from the server.

bashCopy code

Example of configuring browser caching in Apache

apacheCopy code

```
# Example of configuring browser caching in Apache's
.htaccess    file    <IfModule    mod_expires.c>
ExpiresActive On ExpiresByType image/jpeg "access
plus 1 year" ExpiresByType image/png "access plus 1
year" ExpiresByType text/css "access plus 1 year"
```

ExpiresByType application/javascript "access plus 1 year" </IfModule>

In this Apache example, browser caching is configured using the **mod_expires** module. Different file types are assigned expiration dates to control how long they are cached by the browser. Images (JPEG and PNG), CSS files, and JavaScript files are set to be cached for one year. This ensures that these resources are cached locally by the browser, resulting in faster page loads for subsequent visits.

Implementing service workers is another powerful technique for client-side caching, particularly for building progressive web applications (PWAs). Service workers are scripts that run in the background, intercepting and controlling network requests made by the web application. Developers can use service workers to cache static assets, API responses, and other resources, enabling offline functionality and improving performance by serving cached content directly from the client's device.

bashCopy code

Example of registering a service worker in an HTML file

htmlCopy code

```
<!-- Example of registering a service worker in an HTML file --> <script> if ('serviceWorker' in navigator) { window.addEventListener('load', () => { navigator.serviceWorker.register('/service-worker.js') .then(registration => { console.log('Service worker
```

registered:', registration); }) .catch(error => { console.error('Service worker registration failed:', error); }); }); } </script>

In this HTML example, a service worker is registered by checking if the browser supports service workers and then registering the service worker script (**service-worker.js**). Once registered, the service worker can intercept network requests and implement caching strategies to improve offline capabilities and overall performance.

Additionally, client-side storage mechanisms such as local storage and session storage can be utilized to cache data on the client side. Local storage allows developers to store key-value pairs persistently across browser sessions, while session storage provides temporary storage that is cleared when the browser session ends. By storing frequently accessed data in local storage or session storage, developers can reduce the need for server requests and improve the responsiveness of web applications.

javascriptCopy code

```
// Example of storing data in local storage
localStorage.setItem('username', 'john_doe'); // Example of retrieving data from local storage const username = localStorage.getItem('username'); console.log('Username:', username);
```

In this JavaScript example, data is stored in local storage using the **localStorage.setItem()** method and retrieved using the **localStorage.getItem()** method.

Storing data in local storage allows it to persist across browser sessions, enabling efficient caching of user-specific data and preferences.

In summary, client-side caching techniques play a vital role in optimizing web performance and enhancing user experience. By employing strategies such as setting cache-control headers, leveraging browser caching mechanisms, implementing service workers, and utilizing local storage and session storage, developers can effectively cache resources on the client side, reducing server load, minimizing network latency, and improving the responsiveness of web applications. By understanding and implementing these caching techniques, developers can create faster, more efficient, and more responsive web applications that deliver an enhanced user experience.

Server-side caching with AJAX is a crucial technique in modern web development, aimed at improving performance and reducing server load by caching responses from AJAX requests on the server side. This technique involves storing the results of AJAX requests in a cache on the server, allowing subsequent requests for the same data to be served from the cache rather than generating the response dynamically. By leveraging server-side caching with AJAX, developers can significantly enhance the speed and responsiveness of web applications, particularly those that rely heavily on dynamic data fetching.

Implementing server-side caching with AJAX typically involves configuring caching mechanisms on the server, handling cache expiration and invalidation, and ensuring that cached responses are served efficiently to clients.

bashCopy code

Example of setting up server-side caching with AJAX in Node.js with Express.js npm install express

javascriptCopy code

```javascript
// Example of caching AJAX responses on the server side in an Express.js server const express = require('express'); const app = express(); // Define a cache object to store AJAX responses const cache = {}; // Route handler for AJAX requests app.get('/data', (req, res) => { const key = 'data'; // Check if the data is cached if (cache[key]) { console.log('Cached data found'); res.json(cache[key]); } else { console.log('Fetching data from the server'); // Perform AJAX request to fetch data fetchData().then(data => { // Cache the data cache[key] = data; res.json(data); }) .catch(error => { res.status(500).json({ error: 'Internal Server Error' }); }); } }); // Function to simulate fetching data function fetchData() { return new Promise((resolve, reject) => { // Simulate fetching data from a database or external API setTimeout(() => { resolve({ message: 'Data fetched
```

successfully' }); }, 1000); }); } // Define other routes and middleware

In this Node.js example using Express.js, server-side caching of AJAX responses is implemented by maintaining a cache object (**cache**) to store the responses. When an AJAX request is received at the **/data** endpoint, the server first checks if the requested data is cached. If cached data is found, it is served immediately from the cache. Otherwise, the server fetches the data asynchronously, caches it for future requests, and sends the response to the client. This ensures that subsequent requests for the same data are served quickly from the cache, minimizing the need for repeated data retrieval operations.

Server-side caching with AJAX offers several benefits, including reduced server load, improved response times, and enhanced scalability. By caching AJAX responses on the server side, developers can alleviate the burden on backend systems and improve the overall performance of web applications, particularly in scenarios with high traffic volumes or frequent data requests. Additionally, server-side caching helps mitigate the impact of network latency and improves the reliability and responsiveness of web applications, leading to a better user experience.

However, it's essential to consider the cache expiration and invalidation strategies when implementing server-side caching with AJAX. Caches should be configured to expire or invalidate stale data periodically to ensure that clients receive the most up-to-date information. Developers can implement cache expiration policies based on factors such as time-based expiration, data freshness, or changes to underlying data sources. Additionally, cache invalidation mechanisms should be in place to remove outdated or invalid cache entries when data changes occur, preventing clients from receiving stale or inaccurate information.

bashCopy code

Example of cache expiration and invalidation configuration in Express.js

javascriptCopy code

```
// Example of cache expiration and invalidation configuration in an Express.js server const CACHE_TTL = 60 * 60 * 1000; // Cache TTL in milliseconds (1 hour) // Route handler for AJAX requests with cache expiration app.get('/data', (req, res) => { const key = 'data'; // Check if the cached data is expired if (cache[key] && cache[key].timestamp > Date.now() - CACHE_TTL) { console.log('Cached data found and not expired'); res.json(cache[key].data); } else { console.log('Fetching data from the server'); // Perform AJAX request to fetch data fetchData() .then(data => { // Cache the data with timestamp cache[key] = { data, timestamp: Date.now() }; res.json(data); }) .catch(error => {
```

```
res.status(500).json({ error: 'Internal Server Error'
}); }); } });
```

In this modified example, cache expiration and invalidation logic are added to the server-side caching mechanism. Cached data is checked for expiration based on a predefined time-to-live (TTL) value (**CACHE_TTL**), and if the data is expired, it is fetched from the server again. By incorporating cache expiration and invalidation strategies, developers can ensure that cached data remains fresh and accurate, maintaining the integrity of the cache and providing users with reliable and up-to-date information.

In summary, server-side caching with AJAX is a valuable technique for improving the performance, scalability, and reliability of web applications. By caching AJAX responses on the server side, developers can reduce server load, minimize network latency, and enhance the overall user experience. However, it's crucial to implement cache expiration and invalidation strategies to ensure that cached data remains fresh and accurate over time. With careful planning and implementation, server-side caching with AJAX can be an effective tool for optimizing web application performance and delivering high-quality user experiences.

Chapter 7: Progressive Enhancement Techniques

Graceful degradation with AJAX is a crucial concept in web development, particularly in scenarios where JavaScript-enhanced features are implemented to improve user experience. The term refers to the practice of ensuring that web pages remain functional even when JavaScript is disabled or not supported by the user's browser. Graceful degradation is essential for ensuring accessibility and usability for all users, including those with disabilities or older browsers. By implementing graceful degradation techniques, developers can ensure that core functionality remains available, even if advanced features powered by AJAX are not accessible.

One approach to implementing graceful degradation with AJAX is to design web pages using progressive enhancement principles. Progressive enhancement involves creating a basic, functional version of the web page using HTML and CSS, and then adding JavaScript enhancements to improve interactivity and user experience. By following this approach, developers ensure that users with JavaScript disabled can still access essential content and functionality, while those with JavaScript enabled benefit from enhanced features provided by AJAX.

bashCopy code

Example of implementing graceful degradation with AJAX in JavaScript npm install jquery

javascriptCopy code

```javascript
// Example of AJAX request with graceful degradation
if (window.XMLHttpRequest) { // Modern browsers support XMLHttpRequest var xhr = new XMLHttpRequest(); } else { // Fallback for older browsers var xhr = new ActiveXObject("Microsoft.XMLHTTP"); } xhr.onreadystatechange = function() { if (xhr.readyState === XMLHttpRequest.DONE) { if (xhr.status === 200) { // Process AJAX response console.log(xhr.responseText); } else { // Handle error console.error('Error:', xhr.status); } } }; xhr.open('GET', 'https://api.example.com/data', true); xhr.send();
```

In this JavaScript example, an AJAX request is made using the XMLHttpRequest object. The code first checks if the browser supports the XMLHttpRequest object, and if not, falls back to using ActiveXObject for older browsers. By implementing this graceful degradation strategy, the web page remains functional even on browsers that do not support modern AJAX techniques.

Another approach to graceful degradation with AJAX is to provide alternative content or fallbacks for AJAX-powered features. For example, instead of relying solely on JavaScript to load dynamic content,

developers can include static content or server-side rendering as a fallback for users with JavaScript disabled. Additionally, developers can use server-side techniques such as server-side rendering or server-side caching to generate and serve pre-rendered HTML content to users with JavaScript disabled.
javascriptCopy code

```
// Example of providing fallback content for AJAX-powered features var dynamicContent = document.getElementById('dynamic-content'); if (dynamicContent) { // Display loading indicator dynamicContent.innerHTML = '<p>Loading...</p>'; // Make AJAX request fetch('https://api.example.com/data')
.then(response => response.json()).then(data => { // Display dynamic content dynamicContent.innerHTML = '<p>' + data.content + '</p>'; }).catch(error => { // Display error message dynamicContent.innerHTML = '<p>Error: Unable to load content.</p>'; }); }
```

In this JavaScript example, a loading indicator is displayed while the AJAX request is in progress. If the request succeeds, the dynamic content is displayed to the user. However, if the request fails or JavaScript is disabled, an error message or alternative content is displayed instead. This approach ensures that users always have access to relevant content, regardless of their browser's capabilities or JavaScript support.

Additionally, developers can use feature detection techniques to check for support for specific features or APIs before using them in their web applications. Feature detection allows developers to provide alternative functionality or fallbacks for users with browsers that do not support certain features. For example, instead of relying on the Fetch API for AJAX requests, developers can use the XMLHttpRequest object as a fallback for browsers that do not support Fetch.

javascriptCopy code

```javascript
// Example of feature detection for Fetch API support
if (window.fetch) { // Modern browsers support Fetch API fetch('https://api.example.com/data')
.then(response => response.json()) .then(data => {
// Process AJAX response console.log(data); })
.catch(error => { // Handle error
console.error('Error:', error); }); } else { // Fallback
for browsers that do not support Fetch API var xhr =
new XMLHttpRequest(); xhr.onreadystatechange =
function() { if (xhr.readyState ===
XMLHttpRequest.DONE) { if (xhr.status === 200) {
// Process AJAX response
console.log(xhr.responseText); } else { // Handle
error console.error('Error:', xhr.status); } } };
xhr.open('GET', 'https://api.example.com/data',
true); xhr.send(); }
```

In this JavaScript example, feature detection is used to determine whether the browser supports the Fetch API. If Fetch API support is detected, the Fetch API is used to make the AJAX request. However, if the browser does not support the Fetch API, a fallback using the XMLHttpRequest object is provided instead. This ensures that users with older browsers or browsers that do not support the Fetch API can still access the AJAX functionality provided by the web application.

In summary, graceful degradation with AJAX is essential for ensuring accessibility and usability in web applications. By following progressive enhancement principles, providing alternative content or fallbacks for AJAX-powered features, and using feature detection to determine browser capabilities, developers can ensure that web pages remain functional and accessible to all users, regardless of their browser's capabilities or JavaScript support. Graceful degradation with AJAX is a fundamental aspect of web development that helps create inclusive and user-friendly web applications.

Enhancing user experience with progressive enhancement is a fundamental principle in modern web development, focusing on building web applications that are accessible, robust, and performant across a wide range of devices and browsers. Progressive enhancement involves starting with a baseline of core functionality that is universally accessible to all users, regardless of their device capabilities or network conditions, and then layering on additional enhancements for users with more capable devices or modern browsers. This approach ensures that all users can access the basic content and functionality of the web application, while those with more advanced devices or browsers can benefit from enhanced features and experiences.

bashCopy code

Example of implementing progressive enhancement with HTML, CSS, and JavaScript

htmlCopy code

```
<!-- Example of HTML markup with progressive enhancement --> <!DOCTYPE html> <html lang="en"> <head> <meta charset="UTF-8"> <meta name="viewport" content="width=device-width, initial-scale=1.0"> <title>Progressive Enhancement</title> <link rel="stylesheet" href="styles.css"> <script src="script.js" defer></script> </head> <body> <header> <h1>Progressive Enhancement Example</h1> </header> <main> <p>This is the main content of the web page.</p> </main> <footer> <p>&copy; 2024 Progressive Enhancement Example</p> </footer> </body> </html>
```

In this HTML example, progressive enhancement is implemented by starting with semantic HTML markup that provides the basic structure and content of the web page. CSS is then used to enhance the presentation and styling of the content, making it visually appealing and responsive across different screen sizes and devices. Finally, JavaScript is included to add interactivity and additional functionality, such as client-side form validation or dynamic content updates. By structuring the web page in this way, users with older browsers or limited device capabilities can still access and interact with the core content and functionality, while users with more modern browsers or devices can benefit from enhanced features provided by CSS and JavaScript.

One of the key benefits of progressive enhancement is improved accessibility. By starting with a baseline of semantic HTML markup that is well-structured and properly labeled, web developers can ensure that their web applications are accessible to users with disabilities or assistive technologies, such as screen readers. Semantic HTML elements like headings, paragraphs, lists, and links provide meaningful context and navigation cues for all users, enhancing usability and ensuring that content is perceivable and operable by everyone.

bashCopy code

```
# Example of testing web accessibility with Lighthouse
CLI tool npm install -g lighthouse
```

bashCopy code

```
# Command to run Lighthouse accessibility audit
lighthouse https://example.com --view
```

In this example, the Lighthouse CLI tool is used to perform a web accessibility audit on a web application. The **lighthouse** command is used to analyze the accessibility of the specified URL, and the **--view** flag is used to open the audit results in a web browser for review. The audit results provide insights into areas where the web application can be improved to enhance accessibility, such as ensuring proper use of semantic HTML elements, providing descriptive alt text for images, and implementing keyboard navigation and focus management.

Another benefit of progressive enhancement is improved performance and page load times. By delivering a lightweight baseline experience with minimal JavaScript and CSS, web developers can ensure that their web applications load quickly and responsively, even on slower network connections or less powerful devices. As users interact with the web application, additional resources and functionality can be progressively loaded and enhanced, providing a seamless and optimized user experience.

```bash
# Example of lazy loading images with the loading attribute
```

```html
<!-- Example of lazy loading images with the loading attribute --> <img src="placeholder.jpg" data-src="image.jpg" alt="Image" loading="lazy">
```

In this HTML example, the **loading="lazy"** attribute is used to enable lazy loading for an image element. This attribute tells the browser to defer loading of the image until it enters the viewport, improving page load times and reducing the initial load on the network. Lazy loading is particularly useful for web applications with large images or media assets, as it allows users to start interacting with the page content more quickly, while images are loaded in the background as needed.

Additionally, progressive enhancement promotes resilience and future-proofing of web applications. By focusing on building robust, standards-compliant code that degrades gracefully in older browsers or less capable devices, web developers can ensure that their web applications remain functional and accessible over time, even as technologies and device capabilities evolve. As new features and APIs become available, developers can selectively enhance their web applications to take advantage of these advancements, while still providing a consistent and reliable experience for users on older platforms.

bashCopy code

Example of using feature detection with Modernizr JavaScript library npm install modernizr

javascriptCopy code

// Example of feature detection with Modernizr if (Modernizr.geolocation) { // Geolocation API is supported

navigator.geolocation.getCurrentPosition(successCal lback, errorCallback); } else { // Fallback for browsers that do not support Geolocation API alert('Geolocation is not supported by your browser.'); }

In this JavaScript example, the Modernizr library is used to perform feature detection for the Geolocation API. If the browser supports the Geolocation API, the current position of the user is retrieved using **navigator.geolocation.getCurrentPosition()**.

However, if the browser does not support the Geolocation API, a fallback message is displayed to the user. By using feature detection techniques like Modernizr, developers can provide alternative functionality or fallbacks for users with older browsers or less capable devices, ensuring that their web applications remain accessible and functional across a wide range of platforms.

In summary, enhancing user experience with progressive enhancement is essential for creating accessible, resilient, and performant web applications. By starting with a baseline of core functionality and layering on additional enhancements for users with more capable devices or modern browsers, developers can ensure that their web applications are accessible to all users, regardless of their device capabilities or network conditions. Progressive enhancement promotes accessibility, performance, resilience, and future-proofing of web applications, making it a fundamental principle in modern web development.

Chapter 8: AJAX Performance Optimization

Minifying AJAX requests is a vital aspect of optimizing web applications for improved performance and efficiency. When web applications make AJAX requests to fetch data from the server, the response often contains unnecessary characters such as whitespace, comments, and line breaks, which inflate the payload size. Minification involves removing these redundant elements from the response data, resulting in smaller file sizes and faster data transfer between the client and server. This optimization technique is particularly beneficial for reducing latency and improving load times, especially on networks with limited bandwidth or slower connections.

To minify AJAX requests, developers can leverage various tools and libraries that support minification of different types of data, such as JSON, JavaScript, CSS, and HTML. For JSON data, tools like UglifyJS provide CLI commands that enable developers to minify JSON files effortlessly. By running the appropriate command, developers can compress JSON data and produce a minified version with reduced whitespace and comments, thus optimizing the payload size for AJAX responses.

bashCopy code

Example of minifying JSON data using UglifyJS CLI tool uglifyjs input.json -o output.min.json --compress --mangle

In this example, the **uglifyjs** command is used to specify the input JSON file (**input.json**) and the output file for the minified data (**output.min.json**). By including the **--compress** and **--mangle** flags, developers can enable compression and variable name mangling, further reducing the size of the minified JSON file.

Minifying AJAX requests is not limited to JSON data; it can also be applied to other types of responses, such as JavaScript, CSS, and HTML. For JavaScript files, tools like UglifyJS and Terser offer CLI commands to minify JavaScript code efficiently. Similarly, CSS files can be minified using tools like CSSNano, which removes whitespace, comments, and redundant CSS rules to produce a smaller and more optimized CSS file.

bashCopy code

Example of minifying CSS files using CSSNano CLI tool cssnano input.css -o output.min.css

In this example, the **cssnano** command is used to minify a CSS file (**input.css**) and generate a minified version (**output.min.css**). By executing this command, developers can streamline the CSS code by removing unnecessary elements, thereby reducing the file size and enhancing performance when fetching CSS files via AJAX requests.

Additionally, minifying HTML files can further optimize AJAX requests by reducing the size of HTML responses. Tools like HTMLMinifier provide CLI commands to minify HTML code by removing whitespace, comments, and other unnecessary elements. By minifying HTML files, developers can ensure that AJAX responses containing HTML content are compact and efficiently transmitted over the network.

bashCopy code

```
# Example of minifying HTML files using HTMLMinifier CLI tool html-minifier input.html -o output.min.html --collapse-whitespace --remove-comments
```

In this example, the **html-minifier** command is used to minify an HTML file (**input.html**) and generate a minified version (**output.min.html**). By including the **--collapse-whitespace** and **--remove-comments** options, developers can instruct HTMLMinifier to remove whitespace and comments from the HTML code, resulting in a more streamlined and optimized HTML file.

When deploying minified AJAX requests in production environments, it is essential to conduct thorough testing to ensure that the minification process does not impact the functionality or performance of the web application. Developers should monitor network traffic, server load, and user experience metrics to evaluate the effectiveness of minification and identify any potential issues or regressions.

In summary, minifying AJAX requests is a critical optimization technique for improving the performance and efficiency of web applications. By removing unnecessary elements from AJAX responses, such as whitespace, comments, and line breaks, developers can reduce the payload size and enhance data transfer speeds between the client and server. Leveraging CLI commands and tools for minification, developers can streamline JSON, JavaScript, CSS, and HTML files, resulting in faster load times and improved user experience for web applications.

Chapter 9: Integrating AJAX with Websockets

WebSocket is a communication protocol that provides full-duplex communication channels over a single TCP connection, enabling real-time, bidirectional communication between clients and servers. Unlike traditional HTTP requests, which follow a request-response pattern, WebSocket allows servers to push data to clients asynchronously, making it well-suited for applications requiring real-time updates, such as chat applications, live data feeds, and online gaming. Integration of WebSocket with AJAX (Asynchronous JavaScript and XML) allows developers to combine the benefits of both technologies, leveraging AJAX for traditional request-response interactions and WebSocket for real-time communication.

bashCopy code
Example of setting up WebSocket server with Node.js using the ws library npm install ws

javascriptCopy code

```
// Example of WebSocket server setup with Node.js
const WebSocket = require('ws'); const wss = new WebSocket.Server({ port: 8080 });
wss.on('connection', function connection(ws) {
console.log('Client connected'); ws.on('message',
function incoming(message) {
```

```
console.log('Received:   %s',   message); });
ws.send('Hello, client!'); });
```

In this example, the **ws** library is used to create a WebSocket server in Node.js. The **WebSocket.Server** class is instantiated with a specified port number (8080), and the **wss.on('connection')** event handler is used to handle incoming WebSocket connections. When a client connects to the server, the **connection** event is triggered, and a WebSocket connection is established. The server listens for incoming messages from clients using the **ws.on('message')** event handler and sends messages to clients using the **ws.send()** method.

Integration of WebSocket with AJAX involves using WebSocket to establish a persistent connection between the client and server for real-time communication, while still utilizing AJAX for traditional HTTP requests when necessary. By combining these two technologies, developers can create web applications that seamlessly transition between traditional request-response interactions and real-time updates, providing a more dynamic and engaging user experience.

```
javascriptCopy code
// Example of WebSocket integration with AJAX in a web application const ws = new WebSocket('ws://localhost:8080'); ws.onopen = function () { console.log('WebSocket connection established'); }; ws.onmessage = function (event) {
```

```
console.log('Received message:', event.data); //
Update UI with real-time data }; ws.onerror =
function (error) { console.error('WebSocket error:',
error);                    };                    function
sendWebSocketMessage(message)          {          if
(ws.readyState       ===       WebSocket.OPEN)       {
ws.send(message);    console.log('Sent    message:',
message);    }    else    {    console.error('WebSocket
connection not open'); } } // Example of using AJAX
for traditional HTTP requests function fetchData() {
fetch('https://api.example.com/data')
.then(response => response.json()) .then(data => {
console.log('Received data:', data); // Update UI
with    fetched    data    })    .catch(error    =>
console.error('Error fetching data:', error)); }
```

In this example, a WebSocket connection is established with the server using the **WebSocket** constructor, and event handlers are defined to handle various WebSocket events such as **onopen**, **onmessage**, and **onerror**. When a message is received from the server, the **onmessage** event handler is triggered, allowing the client to update its UI with real-time data. The **sendWebSocketMessage()** function demonstrates how clients can send messages to the server over the WebSocket connection.

Additionally, the example illustrates the use of AJAX for traditional HTTP requests using the **fetch()** API. When the **fetchData()** function is called, an HTTP request is made to the specified URL (**https://api.example.com/data**), and the response is parsed as JSON. Once the data is received, the client updates its UI accordingly, demonstrating the integration of AJAX for fetching data from the server.

By integrating WebSocket with AJAX, developers can leverage the strengths of both technologies to create web applications that deliver real-time updates and dynamic content while still supporting traditional HTTP requests when needed. This hybrid approach allows for more responsive and interactive web experiences, making it ideal for a wide range of applications, including collaborative tools, live dashboards, and multiplayer games.

Real-time collaborative applications leverage AJAX (Asynchronous JavaScript and XML) and WebSockets to enable multiple users to work together on shared tasks or projects simultaneously, facilitating seamless communication and collaboration over the internet. These applications range from collaborative text editors and document sharing platforms to real-time multiplayer games and collaborative drawing tools. By combining AJAX for traditional HTTP requests with WebSockets for real-time bidirectional communication, developers can create highly interactive and engaging applications that allow users to collaborate in real time.

To begin building a real-time collaborative application, developers can set up a WebSocket server to handle WebSocket connections from clients and facilitate real-time communication between users. This can be achieved using various programming languages and frameworks that support WebSocket functionality. For instance, Node.js with libraries like Socket.IO or ws provides a robust environment for building WebSocket servers.

bashCopy code

```
# Example of setting up a WebSocket server with Socket.IO in Node.js npm install socket.io
```

javascriptCopy code

```
// Example of setting up a WebSocket server with Socket.IO in Node.js const http = require('http'); const server = http.createServer(); const io = require('socket.io')(server); io.on('connection', (socket) => { console.log('A user connected'); socket.on('message', (data) => { console.log('Message received:', data); // Broadcast the message to all connected clients io.emit('message', data); }); socket.on('disconnect', () => { console.log('A user disconnected'); }); }); server.listen(3000, () => { console.log('WebSocket server listening on port 3000'); });
```

In this example, a WebSocket server is created using Socket.IO, a popular WebSocket library for Node.js. The **io.on('connection')** event handler is used to handle incoming WebSocket connections, and the server listens for messages from clients using the

socket.on('message') event. When a message is received, it is broadcasted to all connected clients using the **io.emit('message')** method. Additionally, the **socket.on('disconnect')** event handler is used to handle disconnections from clients.

Once the WebSocket server is set up, developers can integrate WebSocket functionality into the client-side of the application using JavaScript. This involves establishing a WebSocket connection with the server and handling WebSocket events to send and receive messages in real time.

javascriptCopy code

```
// Example of WebSocket integration in the client-side of a web application const socket = io('http://localhost:3000'); socket.on('connect', () => { console.log('Connected to WebSocket server'); }); socket.on('message', (data) => { console.log('Message received from server:', data); // Update UI with real-time data }); function sendMessage(message) { socket.emit('message', message); }
```

In this example, the client-side JavaScript code establishes a WebSocket connection with the WebSocket server running at **http://localhost:3000** using the **io()** function provided by Socket.IO. Event handlers are defined to handle the **connect** event, indicating a successful connection to the WebSocket server, and the **message** event, which is triggered when a message is received from the server. The

sendMessage() function allows users to send messages to the server over the WebSocket connection.

Integrating AJAX into the real-time collaborative application allows developers to handle traditional HTTP requests for tasks such as fetching initial data, saving changes to the server, and updating content asynchronously. This ensures that the application remains responsive and efficient, even when handling tasks that do not require real-time communication.

javascriptCopy code

```
// Example of using AJAX for fetching initial data in a collaborative application function fetchData() {
fetch('https://api.example.com/data')
.then(response => response.json()) .then(data => {
console.log('Received data:', data); // Update UI with fetched data }) .catch(error =>
console.error('Error fetching data:', error)); }
```

In this example, the **fetchData()** function fetches initial data from a server endpoint (**https://api.example.com/data**) using the Fetch API. Once the data is received, it is parsed as JSON, and the UI is updated accordingly. This demonstrates how AJAX can be used to fetch data asynchronously without blocking the main thread, ensuring a smooth user experience.

By integrating AJAX with WebSockets, developers can create real-time collaborative applications that combine the benefits of both technologies. Users can collaborate in real time, communicate seamlessly, and work together on shared tasks or projects, resulting in a more engaging and productive user experience. Whether it's collaborating on documents, editing code together, or playing multiplayer games, real-time collaborative applications offer endless possibilities for interaction and collaboration over the web.

Chapter 10: Building Responsive AJAX Interfaces

Responsive design principles play a pivotal role in ensuring that AJAX (Asynchronous JavaScript and XML) applications deliver an optimal user experience across various devices and screen sizes. As the usage of mobile devices continues to rise, it's essential for web applications to adapt and provide a seamless experience regardless of the device being used. By adhering to responsive design principles, developers can create AJAX applications that dynamically adjust their layout and content to suit the viewing environment, whether it's a desktop computer, tablet, or smartphone.

To begin implementing responsive design principles in AJAX applications, developers can leverage CSS media queries to apply different styles based on the device's screen size and orientation. Media queries allow developers to specify CSS rules that are only applied when certain conditions are met, such as the width or height of the viewport. This enables the application to adapt its layout and styling dynamically, ensuring that content remains readable and accessible across a wide range of devices.

cssCopy code

```
/* Example of using media queries to create a responsive layout */ @media screen and (max-width: 768px) { /* Styles for smaller screens (e.g.,
```

tablets) */ } @media screen and (max-width: 480px) { /* Styles for even smaller screens (e.g., smartphones) */ }

In this example, media queries are used to define different styles for screens with maximum widths of 768 pixels and 480 pixels, respectively. By adjusting the layout and styling based on the screen size, developers can create a responsive design that optimizes the user experience for both desktop and mobile users.

Another crucial aspect of responsive design for AJAX applications is optimizing the performance of the application, particularly on mobile devices with limited processing power and bandwidth. This involves minimizing the size of resources such as JavaScript files, CSS files, and images to reduce load times and improve performance. Techniques such as minification, compression, and lazy loading can be employed to optimize resource delivery and ensure that the application loads quickly and efficiently on all devices.

bashCopy code

```
# Example of minifying JavaScript files using UglifyJS
CLI tool uglifyjs input.js -o output.min.js --compress --mangle
```

bashCopy code

```
# Example of compressing CSS files using gzip
compression gzip -c input.css > output.min.css.gz
```

In these examples, JavaScript files are minified using the UglifyJS CLI tool, which removes whitespace and renames variables to reduce file size. Similarly, CSS files are compressed using gzip compression to further reduce their size before being served to clients. These optimization techniques help improve the performance of AJAX applications, particularly on mobile devices with slower network connections.

Furthermore, developers should prioritize content and functionality based on the device's capabilities and user needs. This involves adopting a mobile-first approach, where the application's design and functionality are initially optimized for mobile devices and then progressively enhanced for larger screens. By focusing on essential content and functionality for mobile users, developers can ensure that the application remains usable and accessible across all devices, regardless of screen size or input method.

In addition to optimizing layout and performance, developers should also consider touch-friendly design elements and interactions when designing AJAX applications for mobile devices. This includes using larger tap targets, minimizing reliance on hover-based interactions, and optimizing forms and input fields for touch input. By providing a seamless and intuitive user experience on touch-enabled devices, developers can enhance the usability and accessibility of their AJAX applications for mobile users.

cssCopy code

```css
/* Example of styling touch-friendly buttons */
.button { padding: 10px 20px; font-size: 16px;
border-radius: 5px; background-color: #007bff;
color: #ffffff; } .button:hover { background-color:
#0056b3; }
```

In this example, a CSS class is defined to style buttons with larger padding and font size, making them more suitable for touch interactions. Additionally, hover effects are included to provide visual feedback when users interact with the buttons using touch or mouse input.

In summary, responsive design principles are essential for creating AJAX applications that deliver a consistent and optimized user experience across various devices and screen sizes. By leveraging CSS media queries, optimizing performance, prioritizing content and functionality, and incorporating touch-friendly design elements, developers can ensure that their AJAX applications are accessible, usable, and engaging for users on desktop and mobile devices alike.

Touch and gesture support in AJAX interfaces are essential components of modern web applications, facilitating intuitive and interactive user experiences on touch-enabled devices such as smartphones and tablets. As the usage of mobile devices continues to rise, it's crucial for developers to incorporate touch and gesture support into their AJAX interfaces to ensure optimal usability and accessibility across a wide range of devices. By leveraging touch and gesture events provided by browsers and frameworks, developers can create AJAX interfaces that respond seamlessly to touch input, allowing users to navigate, interact, and engage with the application effortlessly.

One fundamental aspect of implementing touch and gesture support in AJAX interfaces is understanding the various touch events provided by web browsers, including touchstart, touchmove, touchend, and touchcancel. These events are triggered when users interact with the touchscreen of their device, enabling developers to capture and respond to touch gestures such as taps, swipes, pinches, and rotations. By listening for these touch events and handling them appropriately, developers can create fluid and responsive user experiences that mimic the behavior of native mobile applications.

javascriptCopy code

```javascript
// Example of handling touch events in a JavaScript-based AJAX interface
element.addEventListener('touchstart', function(event) { // Handle touchstart event });
element.addEventListener('touchmove', function(event) { // Handle touchmove event });
element.addEventListener('touchend', function(event) { // Handle touchend event });
element.addEventListener('touchcancel', function(event) { // Handle touchcancel event });
```

In this example, event listeners are attached to a DOM element to capture touch events such as touchstart, touchmove, touchend, and touchcancel. These event listeners allow developers to respond to touch input and implement custom behavior based on the user's interactions with the interface.

In addition to basic touch events, developers can also leverage gesture events provided by modern web browsers to support more complex touch interactions, such as pinch-to-zoom and rotate. Gesture events like gesturestart, gesturechange, and gestureend provide additional information about multi-touch gestures, enabling developers to create richer and more immersive user experiences in their AJAX interfaces.

javascriptCopy code

```
// Example of handling gesture events in a JavaScript-based AJAX interface
element.addEventListener('gesturestart', function(event) { // Handle gesturestart event });
element.addEventListener('gesturechange', function(event) { // Handle gesturechange event });
element.addEventListener('gestureend', function(event) { // Handle gestureend event });
```

By listening for gesture events and tracking the properties of multi-touch gestures, developers can implement advanced touch interactions that enhance the usability and interactivity of their AJAX interfaces.

Moreover, frameworks and libraries such as jQuery Mobile, Hammer.js, and TouchSwipe provide additional abstractions and utilities for handling touch and gesture input in AJAX interfaces. These frameworks offer pre-built components, gesture recognizers, and event handlers that simplify the process of implementing touch and gesture support, allowing developers to focus on creating engaging user experiences without the need to reinvent the wheel.

bashCopy code

```
# Example of installing Hammer.js library using npm
npm install hammerjs
```

javascriptCopy code

```
// Example of using Hammer.js for touch and gesture support var hammertime = new Hammer(element); hammertime.on('pan', function(event) { // Handle pan gesture }); hammertime.on('pinch', function(event) { // Handle pinch gesture }); hammertime.on('rotate', function(event) { // Handle rotate gesture });
```

In this example, the Hammer.js library is installed using npm, and event listeners are attached to a DOM element to detect and respond to touch and gesture events such as pan, pinch, and rotate. By incorporating Hammer.js into their AJAX interfaces, developers can add support for touch and gesture input with minimal effort, enhancing the overall user experience of their applications.

In summary, touch and gesture support are crucial aspects of modern AJAX interfaces, enabling developers to create intuitive and interactive user experiences that cater to the growing number of users accessing web applications on touch-enabled devices. By leveraging touch events, gesture events, and specialized libraries like Hammer.js, developers can ensure that their AJAX interfaces are responsive, engaging, and accessible across a wide range of devices and input methods, ultimately leading to higher user satisfaction and retention.

BOOK 3
ADVANCED AJAX STRATEGIES
SCALABLE SOLUTIONS FOR COMPLEX WEB
APPLICATIONS

ROB BOTWRIGHT

Chapter 1: AJAX Architecture Patterns

Model-View-Controller (MVC) architecture is a software design pattern commonly used in web development to organize code, separate concerns, and facilitate modular development. The MVC pattern divides an application into three interconnected components: the model, the view, and the controller. Each component has a specific responsibility within the application, promoting code reusability, maintainability, and scalability.

In MVC architecture, the model represents the data and business logic of the application. It encapsulates the application's state and behavior, providing an interface for interacting with and manipulating data. Models are responsible for retrieving data from external sources, performing computations, and enforcing business rules. By centralizing data-related operations within the model layer, developers can ensure consistency and integrity across the application.

bashCopy code

```
# Example of creating a model class in a Node.js application mkdir models touch models/user.js
```

javascriptCopy code

```
// Example of a user model in a Node.js application class User { constructor(id, username, email) { this.id = id; this.username = username; this.email =
```

email; } save() { // Save user data to database } static findById(id) { // Retrieve user data from database by ID } } module.exports = User;

In this example, a User model class is created in a Node.js application to represent user data. The model includes properties such as id, username, and email, as well as methods for saving user data to the database and retrieving user data by ID.

The view layer in MVC architecture is responsible for presenting data to the user and handling user interactions. Views render the user interface based on data provided by the controller and communicate user input back to the controller for processing. Views are typically implemented using templating languages or front-end frameworks, allowing developers to create dynamic and interactive user interfaces that respond to changes in the application's state.

bashCopy code

```bash
# Example of creating a view template in an Express.js application mkdir views touch views/user.ejs
```

htmlCopy code

```html
<!-- Example of a user view template in an Express.js application --> <!DOCTYPE html> <html lang="en"> <head> <meta charset="UTF-8"> <meta name="viewport" content="width=device-width, initial-scale=1.0"> <title>User Profile</title> </head> <body> <h1>User Profile</h1> <p>Username: <%= user.username %></p> <p>Email: <%= user.email %></p> </body> </html>
```

In this example, an EJS (Embedded JavaScript) view template is created in an Express.js application to render a user profile page. The template includes placeholders (<%= user.username %> and <%= user.email %>) that are populated with data provided by the controller.

The controller layer acts as an intermediary between the model and the view, handling user input, processing requests, and coordinating interactions between the model and view. Controllers receive input from the user via the view layer, invoke appropriate methods on the model layer to perform business logic, and pass data to the view layer for rendering. By decoupling the logic for handling user input from the business logic and presentation logic, controllers enable developers to maintain a clear separation of concerns and facilitate code reuse.

```bash
bashCopy code
# Example of creating a controller in a Ruby on Rails
application rails generate controller Users
```

```ruby
rubyCopy code
# Example of a controller in a Ruby on Rails
application class UsersController <
ApplicationController def show @user =
User.find(params[:id]) render 'users/show' end end
```

In this example, a UsersController is generated in a Ruby on Rails application to handle user-related requests. The controller includes an action (show) to retrieve user data from the model layer and render a corresponding view template (users/show).

Overall, MVC architecture provides a structured and modular approach to building web applications, allowing developers to separate concerns, improve code organization, and enhance maintainability. By dividing an application into distinct components (model, view, and controller) with well-defined responsibilities, MVC architecture promotes code reusability, scalability, and collaboration among team members, making it a popular choice for web development projects of all sizes and complexities.

Service-Oriented Architecture (SOA) is a software design paradigm that structures applications as a collection of loosely coupled, interoperable services, each performing a specific function or task. In an SOA, services are self-contained units of functionality that can be accessed and invoked over a network using standardized protocols and communication mechanisms. These services can be deployed independently, allowing for greater flexibility, scalability, and reusability in the development of complex software systems. When combined with AJAX (Asynchronous JavaScript and XML) technology, which enables asynchronous communication between a web browser and a server, SOA offers a powerful approach to building dynamic and interactive web applications that leverage distributed services for data retrieval, processing, and presentation.

The key principle of SOA is the decoupling of services from the underlying implementation details, allowing them to be accessed and consumed independently of the technologies used to implement them. This decoupling enables services to be reused across different applications and platforms, promoting interoperability and integration between disparate systems. By encapsulating functionality within services and exposing them through well-defined interfaces, SOA facilitates the creation of modular, scalable, and maintainable software architectures that can adapt to changing business requirements and technological advancements.

```bash
bashCopy code
# Example of creating a RESTful web service using Node.js and Express.js mkdir services touch services/userService.js
```

```javascript
javascriptCopy code
// Example of a RESTful web service for managing user data in Node.js and Express.js const express = require('express'); const router = express.Router();
// Mock user data let users = [ { id: 1, name: 'John Doe', email: 'john@example.com' }, { id: 2, name: 'Jane Smith', email: 'jane@example.com' }, ]; // Get all users router.get('/', (req, res) => { res.json(users); }); // Get user by ID router.get('/:id', (req, res) => { const userId = parseInt(req.params.id); const user =
```

```
users.find(user => user.id === userId); if (user) {
res.json(user); } else { res.status(404).json({
message: 'User not found' }); } }); module.exports =
router;
```

In this example, a RESTful web service for managing
user data is created using Node.js and Express.js. The
service provides endpoints for retrieving all users and
fetching a user by ID, using HTTP GET requests.

bashCopy code

```
# Example of consuming a RESTful web service using
AJAX in a client-side JavaScript application mkdir
public touch public/index.html
```

htmlCopy code

```
<!-- Example of a client-side JavaScript application
that consumes a RESTful web service using AJAX -->
<!DOCTYPE html> <html lang="en"> <head> <meta
charset="UTF-8">        <meta       name="viewport"
content="width=device-width,      initial-scale=1.0">
<title>User       Management</title>        <script
src="https://code.jquery.com/jquery-
3.6.0.min.js"></script> </head> <body> <h1>User
Management</h1> <ul id="userList"></ul> <script>
$(document).ready(function() { // Fetch all users from
the RESTful web service $.ajax({ url: '/users', method:
'GET',        success:       function(users)        {
users.forEach(function(user)                        {
$('#userList').append(`<li>${user.name}           -
${user.email}</li>`); }); }, error: function(xhr, status,
```

error) { console.error('Error fetching users:', error); }
}); }); </script> </body> </html>

In this example, a client-side JavaScript application is created to consume the RESTful web service for user data. The application uses AJAX to send an HTTP GET request to the '/users' endpoint and displays the list of users returned by the service in an unordered list.

By combining SOA with AJAX, developers can build web applications that leverage distributed services for various functionalities, such as data retrieval, processing, and presentation, while maintaining a high level of flexibility, scalability, and maintainability. SOA allows for the creation of reusable and interoperable services that can be easily integrated into web applications using AJAX technology, enabling developers to build complex and dynamic applications that meet the evolving needs of users and businesses.

Chapter 2: Asynchronous Module Definition (AMD) for AJAX

Implementing Asynchronous Module Definition (AMD) with RequireJS is a fundamental aspect of modern JavaScript development. RequireJS is a popular AMD loader that enables developers to define and manage modules in their web applications. The adoption of AMD and RequireJS has revolutionized the way JavaScript applications are structured and organized, allowing for better code modularity, dependency management, and asynchronous loading of resources. Understanding how to effectively implement AMD with RequireJS is essential for building scalable, maintainable, and performant web applications.

To start using RequireJS in a project, developers typically need to install it using a package manager like npm:

bashCopy code

npm install requirejs

Once installed, developers can create their AMD modules using RequireJS's define function:

javascriptCopy code

```
// Define a module named 'myModule' with
dependencies 'dependency1' and 'dependency2'
define('myModule',          ['dependency1',
'dependency2'],          function(dependency1,
```

dependency2) { // Module implementation return {
// Module exports }; });

In this example, the define function defines a module
named 'myModule' with dependencies 'dependency1'
and 'dependency2'. The dependencies are loaded
asynchronously before the module is executed,
ensuring that the module's dependencies are resolved
before its code is executed.

RequireJS also provides a configuration option to
specify the base URL and paths for modules:

javascriptCopy code

// RequireJS configuration requirejs.config({ baseUrl:
'js', paths: { 'jquery': 'vendor/jquery.min',
'underscore': 'vendor/underscore.min' } });

In this configuration, the baseUrl option specifies the
base URL for module loading, and the paths option
specifies the paths to individual modules. This allows
developers to use short module names in their code
and map them to specific file paths.

One of the key benefits of using RequireJS is its
support for asynchronous module loading. This means
that modules are loaded only when they are needed,
reducing the initial load time of the application and
improving its performance. Additionally, RequireJS
automatically resolves module dependencies and
ensures that they are loaded in the correct order,
simplifying the management of complex dependency
graphs.

Another advantage of RequireJS is its support for dependency injection, which allows developers to inject dependencies into modules at runtime. This promotes loose coupling between modules and makes it easier to test and refactor code.

To optimize the performance of RequireJS-based applications, developers can use the r.js optimizer, which combines and minifies modules into a single file:

bashCopy code

```
r.js -o build.js
```

In the build.js configuration file, developers can specify the entry point module, output file, and other optimization options. This process reduces the number of HTTP requests and file size, resulting in faster page load times and improved performance.

RequireJS also provides a plugin system that extends its functionality and enables developers to load different types of resources, such as text files, JSON data, and CSS files:

javascriptCopy code

```
// Load a text file as a module
define(['text!data.txt'], function(data) { // Module implementation });
```

In this example, the text! plugin is used to load the contents of the data.txt file as a module. This allows developers to include text files in their projects and access them as modules using RequireJS.

Overall, implementing AMD with RequireJS offers several benefits for JavaScript development, including better code organization, improved performance, and enhanced dependency management. By understanding how to effectively use RequireJS in their projects, developers can build more modular, maintainable, and scalable web applications that meet the demands of modern web development.

Chapter 3: AJAX in Single Page Applications (SPA)

Single Page Applications (SPAs) have become increasingly popular in modern web development, offering a seamless and interactive user experience. At the core of SPAs lies the concept of dynamically updating content on a single web page, eliminating the need for traditional page reloads. AJAX (Asynchronous JavaScript and XML) plays a crucial role in SPA development by enabling asynchronous communication between the client and server, facilitating the seamless retrieval and manipulation of data without disrupting the user experience.

SPAs fundamentally differ from traditional multi-page web applications by loading a single HTML page initially and then dynamically updating its content as the user interacts with the application. This approach provides a more responsive and fluid user experience, akin to that of a desktop application. SPAs are typically built using JavaScript frameworks and libraries such as Angular, React, or Vue.js, which offer powerful tools and abstractions for managing application state, routing, and UI components.

To start building an SPA, developers often use a CLI (Command Line Interface) tool provided by their chosen framework or library to scaffold the project structure and set up the initial configuration:

bashCopy code

Example command to create a new React SPA project using Create React App npx create-react-app my-spa cd my-spa

Once the project is set up, developers can begin integrating AJAX functionality to fetch data from a server and update the UI without reloading the page. AJAX requests are typically initiated in response to user interactions or application events, such as clicking a button or navigating to a new route.

javascriptCopy code

```
// Example AJAX request using the Fetch API in a
React component import React, { useState,
useEffect } from 'react'; const MyComponent = ()
=> { const [data, setData] = useState(null);
useEffect(() => { const fetchData = async () => { try
{ const response = await
fetch('https://api.example.com/data'); const
jsonData = await response.json();
setData(jsonData); } catch (error) {
console.error('Error fetching data:', error); } };
fetchData(); }, []); return ( <div> {data ? ( <div>{/*
Render data */}</div> ) : ( <div>Loading...</div> )}
</div> ); }; export default MyComponent;
```

In this example, the Fetch API is used to make an AJAX request to fetch data from an external API. Once the data is retrieved, it is stored in the component's state and used to update the UI accordingly. During the loading state, a placeholder message is displayed to indicate that data is being fetched.

Integrating AJAX into an SPA involves handling various aspects such as error handling, loading indicators, and data caching to ensure a smooth user experience. Error handling is essential to gracefully handle scenarios where AJAX requests fail due to network issues or server errors. Loading indicators are used to provide feedback to users while data is being fetched asynchronously, preventing confusion or frustration. Data caching can improve performance by storing previously fetched data locally and reusing it when applicable, reducing the number of network requests.

javascriptCopy code

```
// Example of error handling in an AJAX request try {
const response = await
fetch('https://api.example.com/data'); if
(!response.ok) { throw new Error('Failed to fetch
data'); } const jsonData = await response.json();
setData(jsonData); } catch (error) {
console.error('Error fetching data:', error); }
```

javascriptCopy code

```
// Example of displaying a loading indicator during an
AJAX request return ( <div> {isLoading ? (
<div>Loading...</div> ) : ( <div>{/* Render data
*/}</div> )} </div> );
```

javascriptCopy code

```javascript
// Example of caching data in local storage
useEffect(() => { const cachedData = localStorage.getItem('cachedData'); if (cachedData) { setData(JSON.parse(cachedData)); } else { fetchData(); } }, []);
```

In addition to fetching data, SPAs often require client-side routing to handle navigation within the application without triggering a full page reload. Routing libraries such as React Router, Vue Router, or Angular Router allow developers to define routes and associated components, enabling seamless navigation between different views within the SPA.

bashCopy code

```bash
# Example command to install React Router for routing in a React SPA npm install react-router-dom
```

javascriptCopy code

```javascript
// Example of defining routes using React Router in a React SPA import { BrowserRouter as Router, Route, Switch } from 'react-router-dom'; import Home from './components/Home'; import About from './components/About'; const App = () => { return ( <Router> <Switch> <Route exact path="/" component={Home} /> <Route path="/about" component={About} /> </Switch> </Router> ); }; export default App;
```

In this example, routes for the home and about pages are defined using React Router's Route component. When a user navigates to a specific route, the corresponding component is rendered without causing a full page reload, providing a seamless navigation experience within the SPA.

Overall, understanding the fundamentals of SPAs and integrating AJAX functionality is essential for building modern web applications that offer a rich and interactive user experience. By leveraging frameworks and libraries that support SPA development, along with best practices for AJAX integration, developers can create powerful and responsive applications that meet the demands of today's users.

Routing and navigation are integral components of Single Page Applications (SPAs), allowing users to seamlessly navigate between different views or pages within the application without the need for full page reloads. With the advent of AJAX (Asynchronous JavaScript and XML), SPAs have become more dynamic and interactive, enabling developers to fetch and render content asynchronously based on user interactions. Implementing routing and navigation in SPAs with AJAX involves managing application state, defining routes, handling navigation events, and updating the UI dynamically.

To begin implementing routing and navigation in an SPA, developers often utilize a routing library or framework specific to their chosen frontend technology. For example, in a React application, developers can use React Router to define routes and handle navigation:

bashCopy code

Install React Router using npm npm install react-router-dom

Once installed, developers can define routes in their application by wrapping components with Route components provided by React Router:

javascriptCopy code

```
// Define routes in a React application using React
Router import { BrowserRouter as Router, Route,
Switch } from 'react-router-dom'; import Home
from './components/Home'; import About from
'./components/About'; const App = () => { return (
<Router> <Switch> <Route exact path="/"
component={Home} /> <Route path="/about"
component={About} /> </Switch> </Router> ); };
export default App;
```

In this example, the BrowserRouter component from React Router is used to provide routing functionality to the application. Route components are used to define different routes, mapping each route to a corresponding component. The Switch component ensures that only one route is rendered at a time, preventing multiple components from being rendered simultaneously.

Once routes are defined, navigation can be implemented using links or programmatic navigation. Links are typically used for navigating between different views within the application:

javascriptCopy code

```javascript
// Example of using links for navigation in a React
component import { Link } from 'react-router-dom';
const Navigation = () => { return ( <nav> <ul>
<li><Link to="/">Home</Link></li> <li><Link
to="/about">About</Link></li> </ul> </nav> ); };
export default Navigation;
```

In this example, the Link component from React Router is used to create navigation links. When a link is clicked, React Router handles the navigation internally, rendering the corresponding route component without causing a full page reload.

In addition to links, programmatic navigation can be achieved using history objects provided by routing libraries. For example, in React Router, developers can use the useHistory hook to access the history object and navigate programmatically:

javascriptCopy code

```javascript
// Example of programmatic navigation in a React
component import { useHistory } from 'react-router-
dom'; const MyComponent = () => { const history =
useHistory(); const handleClick = () => {
history.push('/about'); }; return ( <button
onClick={handleClick}>Go to About</button> ); };
export default MyComponent;
```

In this example, the useHistory hook is used to access the history object, which provides methods like push for navigating to a different route programmatically.

When the button is clicked, the handleClick function is invoked, triggering a navigation to the '/about' route.

Managing application state and updating the UI based on navigation events are also important aspects of routing and navigation in SPAs. For example, developers can use state management libraries like Redux or React Context API to manage global application state and update components dynamically based on route changes.

Overall, routing and navigation in SPAs with AJAX enable developers to create seamless and interactive user experiences by dynamically loading content and updating the UI based on user interactions. By leveraging routing libraries and best practices for navigation, developers can build SPAs that offer a fluid and intuitive navigation experience for users.

Chapter 4: Advanced AJAX Event Handling

Custom event handling in AJAX is a powerful technique that allows developers to create more robust and flexible web applications by defining and dispatching custom events to handle various asynchronous tasks and interactions. While traditional event handling in JavaScript primarily revolves around browser-generated events like click, hover, or submit, custom event handling extends this functionality by enabling developers to define their own events and listeners, providing greater control over application logic and interaction flow.

To implement custom event handling in AJAX, developers typically utilize JavaScript's built-in EventTarget interface, which serves as the base class for objects that can dispatch and listen for events. By extending or instantiating EventTarget objects, developers can define custom events and dispatch them when certain conditions are met. This approach allows for a more modular and decoupled architecture, as different components of the application can communicate through custom events without direct dependencies.

Creating a custom event involves three main steps: defining the event, dispatching the event, and handling the event. Let's explore each step in more detail.

Defining the Event: Before dispatching a custom event, developers need to define the event type and optionally specify additional data to be passed along with the event. This is typically done using the CustomEvent constructor, which accepts the event type as the first argument and an optional configuration object containing additional event data.

javascriptCopy code

```
// Define a custom event named 'dataLoaded' with optional data const event = new CustomEvent('dataLoaded', { detail: { data: { /* Additional data */ } } });
```

Dispatching the Event: Once the custom event is defined, developers can dispatch it on any EventTarget object using the dispatchEvent method. This triggers the execution of any event listeners registered for the specified event type.

javascriptCopy code

```
// Dispatch the custom event on a specific target document.dispatchEvent(event);
```

Handling the Event: To respond to custom events, developers can add event listeners to any EventTarget object using the addEventListener method. When the specified event type is dispatched, the associated event listener function is invoked, allowing developers to execute custom logic based on the event.

javascriptCopy code

```
// Handle the custom event by adding an event
listener    document.addEventListener('dataLoaded',
(event) => { const eventData = event.detail.data; //
Perform actions based on the event data });
```

By adopting custom event handling in AJAX,
developers can achieve greater flexibility and
modularity in their codebase, leading to improved
maintainability and scalability. For example, in a web
application that fetches data asynchronously using
AJAX, custom events can be used to notify
components when the data has been successfully
loaded, allowing them to update their UI accordingly
without tight coupling between components.

In practical scenarios, custom event handling in AJAX
can be applied to various use cases, such as:

Notifying components of successful or failed AJAX
requests.

Triggering UI updates based on changes in application
state.

Implementing custom interactions and workflows
within the application.

Communicating between different modules or layers
of the application architecture.

Moreover, custom event handling can be particularly
useful in larger and more complex applications where
maintaining clear separation of concerns and
minimizing dependencies is essential for long-term
maintainability. By encapsulating logic within event
listeners and dispatching events to trigger specific
actions, developers can create more modular and

reusable code, facilitating easier collaboration and code maintenance across teams.

In summary, custom event handling in AJAX is a versatile technique that empowers developers to create more dynamic and interactive web applications by defining custom events, dispatching them as needed, and handling them with event listeners. By embracing custom event handling, developers can achieve greater flexibility, modularity, and maintainability in their codebase, ultimately enhancing the overall user experience of their web applications.

Event delegation is a powerful concept in web development, particularly in AJAX applications, where dynamic content may be added or removed from the DOM dynamically. It's a technique that involves attaching event handlers to a parent element rather than individual child elements. This allows for more efficient event handling, especially in scenarios where there are numerous child elements or when elements are added or removed dynamically.

To understand event delegation in AJAX applications, let's delve into its implementation and benefits.

One of the primary advantages of event delegation is its ability to handle events on dynamically added elements without the need to reattach event handlers manually. This is particularly useful in AJAX applications where content is loaded asynchronously, and new elements are added to the DOM dynamically. Instead of attaching event handlers to each new element individually, developers can attach event handlers to a parent element that exists in the DOM from the start. This ensures that events are captured even on elements added after the initial page load.

The process of implementing event delegation involves selecting a parent element that will serve as the container for delegated events and attaching event handlers to it. When an event occurs on a child element within the container, the event bubbles up the DOM tree to the parent element, where the event handler is invoked.

For example, consider a scenario where a list of items is loaded dynamically via AJAX, and each item has a click event associated with it. Instead of attaching a click event handler to each item individually, developers can attach a single click event handler to the parent container element, such as a <ul> or <div>, using JavaScript.

javascriptCopy code

```
// Select the parent container element const
container = document.getElementById('container');
// Add event listener for click events
container.addEventListener('click', function(event)
{ // Check if the clicked element is an item within the
container if (event.target.classList.contains('item'))
{ // Handle the click event on the item
```

```
console.log('Item                    clicked:',
event.target.textContent); } });
```

In this example, the click event is delegated to the parent container element ('container'). When a click event occurs on any child element within the container, the event bubbles up to the container, and the event handler checks if the clicked element has the class 'item' (representing individual list items). If the clicked element is an item, the event is handled accordingly.

Event delegation not only simplifies event handling in AJAX applications but also improves performance by reducing the number of event handlers attached to the DOM. Instead of attaching event handlers to every individual element, developers can attach a single event handler to a parent container, resulting in cleaner and more efficient code.

Moreover, event delegation enables developers to handle events for elements that may not exist in the DOM at the time the event handler is attached. This is particularly useful in scenarios where elements are dynamically added or removed based on user interactions or data updates.

Another benefit of event delegation is its ability to improve memory management in JavaScript applications. Since event handlers are attached to a single parent element rather than multiple child elements, memory usage is optimized, leading to better performance and smoother user experience, especially in applications with large DOM structures.

In addition to click events, event delegation can be applied to various other types of events, such as mouseover, mouseout, change, and keyup events, allowing for more comprehensive event handling in AJAX applications.

Overall, event delegation is a fundamental technique in web development, especially in AJAX applications, where dynamic content manipulation is prevalent. By attaching event handlers to parent container elements, developers can simplify event handling, improve performance, and enhance the scalability of their applications. Event delegation is a versatile and efficient approach that empowers developers to create more responsive and interactive user experiences in AJAX applications.

Chapter 5: AJAX for Cross-Platform Development

Responsive design has become a critical aspect of modern web development, particularly in the context of AJAX applications aiming for cross-platform compatibility. It's a design approach that ensures web applications adapt seamlessly to various devices and screen sizes, providing users with an optimal viewing experience regardless of the device they are using. In the realm of AJAX applications, where content is loaded dynamically and interactions are often asynchronous, responsive design plays a vital role in ensuring usability and accessibility across different platforms and devices.

To achieve responsive design in cross-platform AJAX applications, developers employ a combination of techniques and best practices aimed at creating flexible and adaptable user interfaces. These techniques include fluid layouts, media queries, flexible images, and scalable vectors, among others. By leveraging these techniques, developers can design web applications that respond intuitively to changes in screen size and orientation, providing users with a consistent and enjoyable experience across desktops, tablets, and smartphones.

One of the fundamental principles of responsive design is the use of fluid layouts, which allow web applications to adjust their layout dynamically based on the available screen real estate. Instead of fixed-width layouts that may appear cramped or distorted on smaller screens, fluid layouts expand and contract fluidly to accommodate different screen sizes. This ensures that content remains readable and accessible regardless of the device being used.

Media queries are another essential aspect of responsive design, enabling developers to apply specific styles based on the characteristics of the user's device, such as screen width, height, orientation, and pixel density. By defining breakpoints within their CSS code, developers can tailor the appearance of their web applications to different devices, optimizing layout, typography, and navigation for each screen size.

For example, developers can use media queries to adjust the font size, spacing, and positioning of elements on smaller screens to improve readability and usability. Additionally, media queries can be used to hide or show certain elements selectively based on screen size, ensuring a streamlined and focused user experience across devices.

Flexible images and scalable vectors are also essential components of responsive design, allowing developers to ensure that images and graphics adapt smoothly to different screen sizes without loss of quality or distortion. By using relative units such as percentages or ems to specify image dimensions, developers can create images that resize proportionally based on the size of the viewport, maintaining clarity and visual appeal across devices.

In the context of AJAX applications, responsive design becomes even more critical due to the dynamic nature of content loading and interaction. Developers must ensure that asynchronous updates and interactions are handled gracefully across devices, maintaining performance and usability regardless of network conditions or device capabilities.

One common approach to achieving responsive design in AJAX applications is to prioritize content and interactions based on device capabilities and user context. For example, on smaller screens, developers may choose to simplify navigation, prioritize essential content, and optimize interactions for touch input to enhance usability on touchscreen devices. On larger screens, additional features and functionalities may be made available to take advantage of the increased screen real estate and input methods such as mouse and keyboard.

To deploy responsive design techniques in cross-platform AJAX applications, developers can use a variety of tools and frameworks that provide built-in support for responsive design principles. For instance, popular frontend frameworks like Bootstrap and Foundation offer responsive grid systems, components, and utilities that streamline the development of responsive web applications. By leveraging these frameworks, developers can rapidly prototype and build cross-platform AJAX applications with responsive layouts and components out of the box.

Moreover, CSS preprocessors like Sass and Less enable developers to write more maintainable and scalable stylesheets by using variables, mixins, and functions. This allows for easier management of media queries and responsive styles, making it simpler to create consistent and adaptive designs across different screen sizes and devices.

In summary, responsive design is essential for creating cross-platform AJAX applications that deliver a consistent and user-friendly experience across devices. By employing fluid layouts, media queries, flexible images, and scalable vectors, developers can design web applications that adapt seamlessly to various screen sizes and orientations, ensuring usability and accessibility for all users. Additionally, leveraging tools and frameworks that support responsive design principles can expedite the development process and facilitate the creation of responsive and engaging AJAX applications.

Frameworks play a crucial role in modern web development, providing developers with pre-built components, libraries, and tools to streamline the development process. When it comes to cross-platform AJAX development, choosing the right framework is essential for building robust, scalable, and maintainable web applications that work seamlessly across different devices and platforms.

Next, we'll explore some of the popular frameworks used for cross-platform AJAX development and how they facilitate the creation of dynamic and responsive web applications.

One of the most widely adopted frameworks for cross-platform AJAX development is AngularJS, developed and maintained by Google. AngularJS is an open-source JavaScript framework that enables developers to build dynamic single-page applications (SPAs) with ease. It provides a comprehensive set of features, including data binding, dependency injection, and routing, making it ideal for building complex and interactive web applications.

To get started with AngularJS, developers can use the Angular CLI (Command Line Interface), a command-line tool for scaffolding and managing Angular projects. By running the following command in the terminal:

arduinoCopy code

ng new my-angular-app

Developers can create a new Angular project with the necessary directory structure and configuration files pre-configured. They can then use the Angular CLI to generate components, services, and other artifacts, making it easier to organize and manage their codebase.

Another popular framework for cross-platform AJAX development is React, developed by Facebook. React is a JavaScript library for building user interfaces, with a focus on component-based architecture and declarative programming. It's widely used for building interactive and responsive web applications, including SPAs and progressive web apps (PWAs).

To create a new React project, developers can use Create React App, a command-line tool that sets up a new React project with a minimal configuration. By running the following command:

luaCopy code

```
npx create-react-app my-react-app
```

Developers can bootstrap a new React project in minutes, complete with a development server, build scripts, and project structure. Create React App also provides a built-in development server with hot module replacement, allowing developers to see changes in real-time as they edit their code.

Vue.js is another popular framework for cross-platform AJAX development, known for its simplicity and ease of use. Vue.js is a progressive JavaScript framework that focuses on the view layer, making it easy to integrate with other libraries and existing projects. It's often compared to AngularJS and React but offers a more lightweight and flexible approach to building web applications.

To create a new Vue.js project, developers can use Vue CLI, a command-line tool for scaffolding Vue.js projects. By running the following command:

luaCopy code

```
vue create my-vue-app
```

Developers can generate a new Vue.js project with various options for configuration and features. Vue

CLI provides a guided setup process that allows developers to choose the features they need, such as TypeScript support, router integration, and state management.

In addition to these mainstream frameworks, there are also specialized frameworks and libraries tailored specifically for AJAX development. For example, Axios is a popular JavaScript library for making HTTP requests from the browser, providing a simple and intuitive API for handling AJAX requests and responses.

To use Axios in a project, developers can include it as a dependency using a package manager like npm or Yarn. By running the following command:

Copy code

npm install axios

Developers can add Axios to their project and start making AJAX requests immediately. Axios supports various features such as request and response interception, automatic JSON parsing, and error handling, making it a versatile choice for AJAX development.

Another notable library for AJAX development is jQuery, a fast, small, and feature-rich JavaScript library. While jQuery is often associated with DOM manipulation and event handling, it also includes a comprehensive set of AJAX functions for making HTTP requests, handling JSON data, and performing other AJAX-related tasks.

To include jQuery in a project, developers can either download it from the official website or include it via a content delivery network (CDN). Once included in the project, developers can use jQuery's AJAX functions, such as $.ajax(), $.get(), and $.post(), to interact with remote servers and fetch data asynchronously.

Overall, choosing the right framework or library for cross-platform AJAX development depends on various factors, including project requirements, developer preferences, and the specific use case. Whether it's AngularJS, React, Vue.js, Axios, or jQuery, each framework and library offers unique features and benefits for building dynamic and responsive web applications that work seamlessly across different platforms and devices. By leveraging the capabilities of these frameworks and libraries, developers can accelerate the development process, improve code maintainability, and deliver exceptional user experiences in their AJAX applications.

Chapter 6: Managing State in AJAX Applications

Client-side state management is a crucial aspect of modern web development, particularly in the context of single-page applications (SPAs) and complex web applications that rely heavily on client-side interactions and dynamic content. Next, we'll explore various techniques and strategies for managing state on the client side, including local storage, session storage, cookies, and state management libraries.

One of the simplest and most commonly used techniques for client-side state management is local storage. Local storage is a web storage API that allows developers to store key-value pairs locally in the user's browser. Data stored in local storage persists even after the browser is closed and reopened, making it ideal for storing small amounts of persistent data such as user preferences, authentication tokens, and application settings.

To store data in local storage using JavaScript, developers can use the localStorage object, which provides methods for setting and retrieving data. For example, to store a user's preferences in local storage, developers can use the following code:

javascriptCopy code

```
// Store user preferences in local storage
localStorage.setItem('theme', 'dark');
```

And to retrieve the stored data:

javascriptCopy code

// Retrieve user preferences from local storage const theme = localStorage.getItem('theme');

Another web storage API that can be used for client-side state management is session storage. Session storage is similar to local storage but scoped to the current browser session. Data stored in session storage persists only for the duration of the session and is automatically cleared when the session ends, typically when the user closes the browser tab or window.

To store data in session storage, developers can use the sessionStorage object, which works similarly to localStorage. For example, to store temporary user data in session storage:

javascriptCopy code

// Store temporary user data in session storage sessionStorage.setItem('userId', '123456');

And to retrieve the stored data:

javascriptCopy code

// Retrieve temporary user data from session storage const userId = sessionStorage.getItem('userId');

Cookies are another commonly used mechanism for client-side state management. Cookies are small pieces of data sent by a website and stored in the user's browser. They can be used to store user preferences, authentication tokens, and other stateful information.

To set a cookie using JavaScript, developers can use the document.cookie property, which allows them to set key-value pairs and specify additional attributes such as expiration date, domain, and path. For example, to set a cookie named "username" with a value of "john.doe":

javascriptCopy code

```
// Set a cookie named "username" with value "john.doe" document.cookie = 'username=john.doe; expires=Thu, 18 Dec 2025 12:00:00 UTC; path=/';
```

And to retrieve the value of a cookie:

javascriptCopy code

```
// Retrieve the value of the "username" cookie const cookies = document.cookie.split('; '); const usernameCookie = cookies.find(cookie => cookie.startsWith('username=')); const username = usernameCookie ? usernameCookie.split('=')[1] : null;
```

While local storage, session storage, and cookies are suitable for storing small amounts of data, they have limitations in terms of storage capacity and security. For more complex state management requirements, developers often turn to state management libraries such as Redux, MobX, and Vuex.

Redux is a popular state management library for JavaScript applications, particularly those built with React. It follows the principles of a unidirectional data flow and immutable state, making it easy to reason about application state and track changes over time.

Redux stores application state in a single immutable object called the store, and developers can use actions and reducers to update the state in a predictable and controlled manner.

To integrate Redux into a React application, developers can use the Redux Toolkit, which provides a set of tools and utilities for simplifying Redux setup and reducing boilerplate code. To create a Redux store with Redux Toolkit:

bashCopy code

```
npm install @reduxjs/toolkit
```

javascriptCopy code

```
// Import necessary modules import { configureStore } from '@reduxjs/toolkit'; // Define initial state and reducers const initialState = { counter: 0, }; const counterReducer = (state = initialState, action) => { switch (action.type) { case 'increment': return { ...state, counter: state.counter + 1 }; case 'decrement': return { ...state, counter: state.counter - 1 }; default: return state; } }; // Create Redux store const store = configureStore({ reducer: counterReducer, });
```

MobX is another popular state management library for JavaScript applications, known for its simplicity and flexibility. Unlike Redux, which relies on actions and reducers, MobX uses observables and reactions to track state changes and trigger updates. MobX provides a more imperative and reactive approach to state management, making it well-suited for applications with complex and dynamic state requirements.

To integrate MobX into a JavaScript application, developers can install the MobX package and use decorators to define observable state and actions. For example, to create a simple counter store with MobX:

Synchronizing state between the client and server is a critical aspect of web development, particularly in applications where real-time updates and collaboration are required. Next, we'll delve into various techniques and strategies for achieving synchronization between the client and server, ensuring that both sides of the application maintain a consistent and up-to-date view of the data.

One of the fundamental approaches to synchronizing state between the client and server is through the use of AJAX requests. AJAX (Asynchronous JavaScript and XML) allows web applications to send and receive data from a server asynchronously without interfering with the current page's behavior. By making AJAX requests, the client can fetch updates from the server and reflect changes in the user interface without requiring a full page reload.

To initiate an AJAX request from the client side, developers can use the XMLHttpRequest object in vanilla JavaScript or utilize modern libraries and frameworks such as Axios or Fetch API. For example, to fetch data from a server using Fetch API:

javascriptCopy code

```
// Perform an AJAX GET request to fetch data from
the server fetch('/api/data') .then(response =>
response.json()) .then(data => { // Handle the
received data  console.log(data); }) .catch(error => {
// Handle errors  console.error('Error fetching data:',
error); });
```

On the server side, developers need to implement endpoints or APIs to handle incoming AJAX requests, process data, and respond with the appropriate data or updates. This often involves using server-side technologies such as Node.js with Express, Django, Flask, or other backend frameworks to define routes and controllers for handling requests.

In addition to fetching data from the server, AJAX requests can also be used to send data from the client to the server, allowing users to update information or perform actions that modify the application's state. For example, to send form data to the server for processing:

javascriptCopy code

```
// Perform an AJAX POST request to send form data
to the server fetch('/api/submit', { method: 'POST',
headers: { 'Content-Type': 'application/json' }, body:
JSON.stringify(formData)  }) .then(response =>
response.json()) .then(data => { // Handle the
response from the server  console.log(data); })
```

```
.catch(error    =>    {    //    Handle    errors
```
console.error('Error submitting form:', error); });

Once the server receives the data, it can process the request, update the state, and send back a response to confirm the action's success or failure.

Another approach to synchronizing state between the client and server is through the use of websockets. Websockets provide a bidirectional communication channel between the client and server, enabling real-time data transfer and updates without the need for continuous polling or repeated AJAX requests.

To implement websockets in a web application, developers can use libraries such as Socket.io (for Node.js) or WebSocket API (for browser-based applications). With websockets, the server can push updates to connected clients instantly, allowing for seamless real-time collaboration and synchronization of state across multiple clients.

For example, using Socket.io in a Node.js server:

javascriptCopy code

```
const    io    =    require('socket.io')(server);
io.on('connection', (socket) => { console.log('A client connected'); // Handle incoming messages from the client socket.on('message', (data) => { console.log('Message received:', data); // Broadcast the message to all connected clients io.emit('message', data); }); // Handle disconnection
```

```javascript
socket.on('disconnect', () => { console.log('A client
disconnected'); }); });
```
And on the client side:

javascriptCopy code
```javascript
// Connect to the websocket server const socket =
io(); // Send a message to the server
socket.emit('message', 'Hello, server!'); // Listen for
incoming messages from the server
socket.on('message', (data) => {
console.log('Message from server:', data); });
```

With websockets, any changes made to the application's state on the server can be instantly propagated to all connected clients, ensuring a synchronized view of the data across the entire application.

In summary, synchronizing state between the client and server is crucial for maintaining consistency and real-time updates in web applications. Through techniques such as AJAX requests and websockets, developers can achieve seamless communication between the client and server, enabling efficient data transfer and synchronization of state across distributed systems.

Chapter 7: Microservices Integration with AJAX

Microservices architecture has emerged as a leading approach for designing and building modern, scalable, and flexible software systems. Next, we will explore the fundamental concepts, principles, benefits, and challenges of microservices architecture.

At its core, microservices architecture is a design paradigm that structures an application as a collection of small, loosely coupled, and independently deployable services, each responsible for a specific business capability. Unlike traditional monolithic architectures, where all functionality is tightly integrated into a single codebase and deployed as a single unit, microservices break down the application into smaller, more manageable components, each with its own codebase, data storage, and communication mechanisms.

One of the key principles of microservices architecture is the idea of bounded contexts, which defines the scope and boundaries of each service. Each microservice is responsible for a distinct business domain or functionality, encapsulating its own data and logic. This isolation allows teams to develop, deploy, and scale individual services independently, without affecting other parts of the system.

To illustrate the concept of microservices architecture, let's consider an e-commerce application. Instead of building a monolithic application that handles everything from product catalog management to order processing in a single codebase, a microservices approach would involve breaking down the application into smaller services such as product catalog service, order service, payment service, and user management service. Each service can be developed, deployed, and scaled independently, enabling faster development cycles, improved agility, and better fault isolation.

One of the primary benefits of microservices architecture is its scalability. By decomposing the application into smaller services, organizations can scale individual components horizontally or vertically based on demand, without having to scale the entire system. This granular scalability allows for more efficient resource utilization and better performance under heavy loads.

Moreover, microservices architecture promotes flexibility and agility in software development. Since each service is independent and has its own codebase, development teams can choose the most appropriate technology stack, programming languages, and frameworks for each service, based on its specific requirements. This polyglot approach enables organizations to leverage the strengths of different technologies and adapt to changing business needs more effectively.

Additionally, microservices architecture fosters a culture of continuous delivery and DevOps practices. With smaller, more manageable services, teams can release new features, updates, and bug fixes more frequently, without the risk of disrupting the entire system. Continuous integration and deployment pipelines can be implemented for each service, enabling automated testing, deployment, and monitoring, leading to faster time-to-market and improved software quality.

However, despite its many benefits, microservices architecture also presents several challenges and complexities. One of the main challenges is managing the complexity of distributed systems. With multiple services communicating over the network, developers need to handle issues such as service discovery, load balancing, fault tolerance, and inter-service communication. Tools and technologies such as service meshes, API gateways, and message brokers can help address these challenges, but they introduce additional complexity to the architecture.

Another challenge is ensuring data consistency and integrity across distributed services. In a microservices environment, each service typically has its own database or data store, which can lead to data duplication, inconsistency, and synchronization issues. Implementing distributed transactions or using eventual consistency patterns can help mitigate these challenges, but they add complexity to the application logic and increase the risk of data anomalies.

Furthermore, managing the deployment and operation of a large number of microservices can be challenging. Organizations need robust infrastructure automation, container orchestration, and monitoring tools to effectively deploy, scale, and manage microservices in production environments. Containerization technologies such as Docker and container orchestration platforms like Kubernetes have become essential components of microservices deployments, enabling organizations to achieve scalability, resilience, and portability across different environments.

In summary, microservices architecture offers many benefits in terms of scalability, flexibility, and agility, but it also introduces complexities and challenges in terms of distributed system management, data consistency, and operational overhead. By understanding the core principles and best practices of microservices architecture and leveraging appropriate tools and technologies, organizations can successfully design, implement, and operate microservices-based systems that meet the needs of modern software development and deployment.

Implementing microservices communication with AJAX involves establishing communication channels between microservices to enable seamless interaction and data exchange in a distributed system architecture. AJAX, or Asynchronous JavaScript and XML, is a powerful technology commonly used for making asynchronous HTTP requests from the client-side to the server. While traditionally associated with frontend development, AJAX can also play a crucial role in facilitating communication between microservices in modern web applications.

To begin implementing microservices communication with AJAX, developers first need to identify the various microservices involved in the system and determine the communication patterns required to fulfill business requirements. Microservices typically communicate with each other over the network using APIs, messaging protocols, or event-driven mechanisms. AJAX can be employed to consume these APIs and exchange data between microservices asynchronously, enabling responsive and efficient communication.

The XMLHttpRequest (XHR) object is the core component of AJAX, allowing JavaScript to make HTTP requests to a server and handle the responses asynchronously. To initiate an HTTP request using AJAX in a web application, developers can use the **XMLHttpRequest** constructor to create a new instance of the XHR object. For example, in JavaScript code, the following command creates a new XMLHttpRequest object:

csharpCopy code

```
var xhr = new XMLHttpRequest();
```

Once the XHR object is created, developers can configure the request parameters such as the HTTP method, URL, headers, and payload data before sending the request to the server. For instance, to send a GET request to retrieve data from a microservice endpoint, developers can specify the request method and URL as follows:

kotlinCopy code

```
xhr.open('GET', 'https://api.example.com/data', true);
```

After configuring the request, developers can set up event listeners to handle different stages of the AJAX request lifecycle, such as when the request is successfully completed, encounters an error, or progresses during transmission. Event listeners such as **onreadystatechange**, **onload**, **onerror**, and **onprogress** can be attached to the XHR object to execute custom JavaScript code when these events occur. For example, to handle the response data returned by the server, developers can define an **onload** event listener as follows:

javascriptCopy code

```
xhr.onload = function() { if (xhr.status === 200) { // Process the response data var responseData = JSON.parse(xhr.responseText);
console.log('Response:', responseData); } else { // Handle error response console.error('Request failed with status:', xhr.status); } };
```

Once the event listeners are set up, developers can initiate the AJAX request by calling the **send()** method on the XHR object. This method sends the HTTP request to the server asynchronously, allowing the client-side code to continue executing while waiting for the server's response. For example, to send the configured GET request, developers can call the **send()** method as follows:

scssCopy code

xhr.send();

Upon receiving the response from the server, the event listeners attached to the XHR object are triggered, allowing developers to process the response data, handle errors, and update the user interface accordingly. Depending on the application requirements, developers may need to implement error handling, data validation, and response parsing logic to ensure robust communication between microservices.

In addition to traditional AJAX techniques using the XHR object, modern web development frameworks such as React, Angular, and Vue.js offer higher-level abstractions and libraries for making HTTP requests and managing asynchronous data fetching in microservices-based applications. These frameworks provide built-in features for handling AJAX requests, managing state, and updating the UI based on the server's response, simplifying the development process and improving code maintainability.

Furthermore, developers can leverage AJAX in conjunction with other communication protocols and technologies such as WebSockets, GraphQL, and RESTful APIs to implement more advanced communication patterns and support real-time updates, bidirectional data exchange, and efficient resource utilization in microservices architectures.

Overall, implementing microservices communication with AJAX involves utilizing the XMLHttpRequest object or modern web frameworks to make asynchronous HTTP requests, handle server responses, and facilitate data exchange between microservices in distributed systems. By understanding the fundamentals of AJAX and applying best practices in web development, developers can build robust and scalable microservices-based applications that meet the evolving needs of modern software architectures.

Chapter 8: Real-time Collaboration with AJAX

Collaborative editing with AJAX revolutionizes the way users interact with web applications by enabling real-time, simultaneous editing of shared documents or content by multiple users from different locations. This advanced functionality enhances productivity and facilitates seamless collaboration among team members or participants working on collaborative projects or documents. AJAX, or Asynchronous JavaScript and XML, plays a pivotal role in enabling real-time updates and synchronization of changes across all connected clients, ensuring a smooth and responsive editing experience.

To implement collaborative editing with AJAX, developers utilize a combination of client-side and server-side technologies to manage the editing process and synchronize changes in real-time. The process involves establishing a WebSocket connection between the client and server to facilitate bidirectional communication, allowing clients to send and receive updates as users edit the shared content. WebSocket is a communication protocol that provides full-duplex communication channels over a single, long-lived TCP connection, making it ideal for real-time applications such as collaborative editing.

To initiate a WebSocket connection in a web application, developers can use the WebSocket API provided by modern web browsers or WebSocket libraries/frameworks in JavaScript. For instance, in JavaScript code, developers can create a new WebSocket instance and specify the WebSocket server's URL as follows:

csharpCopy code

```
var socket = new WebSocket('ws://example.com/socket');
```

Upon establishing the WebSocket connection, clients can send messages to the server or receive messages from the server using event handlers such as **onopen**, **onmessage**, **onclose**, and **onerror**. Developers can define custom logic in these event handlers to handle various stages of the WebSocket connection lifecycle, including connection establishment, message reception, connection closure, and error handling.

For collaborative editing, when a user makes changes to the shared document or content, the client sends the edited content or changes to the server using the WebSocket connection. The server receives the updates from the client, processes the changes, and broadcasts the updated content to all connected clients in real-time. This process ensures that all users viewing or editing the shared document receive instant updates and see the changes made by other participants in real-time, creating a collaborative editing environment.

In addition to WebSocket, AJAX techniques such as long polling or server-sent events (SSE) can also be used to implement collaborative editing features in web applications. Long polling involves making periodic HTTP requests to the server to check for updates or changes, while SSE enables the server to push updates to clients over a single, long-lived HTTP connection. While WebSocket offers low-latency, bidirectional communication, long polling and SSE provide alternatives for environments where WebSocket support may be limited or unavailable.

To handle collaborative editing conflicts or concurrent edits by multiple users, developers can implement conflict resolution algorithms or operational transformation techniques on the server-side to reconcile conflicting changes and ensure data consistency across all clients. These techniques analyze the changes made by each user, resolve conflicts based on predefined rules or policies, and synchronize the edited content to maintain a consistent state across all clients.

Furthermore, to enhance the collaborative editing experience, developers can implement additional features such as real-time cursors, presence indicators, and revision history tracking. Real-time cursors display the position of each user's cursor or caret in the shared document, allowing users to see where others are editing in real-time. Presence indicators indicate the online/offline status of connected users, enabling users to see who else is currently active in the document. Revision history tracking records and displays the sequence of changes made to the document over time, allowing users to review, revert, or undo changes as needed.

In summary, collaborative editing with AJAX transforms traditional web applications into powerful collaboration platforms, enabling multiple users to edit shared documents or content simultaneously in real-time. By leveraging WebSocket connections, AJAX techniques, and conflict resolution strategies, developers can build robust and responsive collaborative editing features that enhance productivity and facilitate seamless collaboration among users in web-based environments.

Real-time messaging and notifications are integral components of modern web applications, providing users with instant updates, alerts, and communication capabilities. These features enhance user engagement, facilitate seamless communication, and enable timely delivery of information across various platforms and devices. Leveraging technologies such as WebSockets, server-sent events (SSE), and push notifications, developers can implement real-time messaging and notification systems that deliver content and updates to users in real-time, creating dynamic and interactive user experiences.

To implement real-time messaging and notifications in a web application, developers often utilize WebSocket technology to establish a persistent, bidirectional communication channel between the client and server. This enables real-time data exchange and enables instant updates to be pushed from the server to connected clients without the need for frequent HTTP polling. Using the WebSocket API in JavaScript, developers can initiate a WebSocket connection by creating a new WebSocket instance and specifying the WebSocket server's URL:

csharpCopy code

```csharp
var socket = new WebSocket('ws://example.com/socket');
```

Once the WebSocket connection is established, clients can send messages to the server or receive messages from the server using event handlers such as **onopen**, **onmessage**, **onclose**, and **onerror**. This allows developers to implement custom logic to handle various aspects of the WebSocket connection lifecycle, including connection establishment, message reception, connection closure, and error handling.

In addition to WebSocket, server-sent events (SSE) provide an alternative mechanism for delivering real-time updates from the server to the client over a single, long-lived HTTP connection. Unlike WebSocket, which facilitates bidirectional communication, SSE enables the server to push updates to the client in a unidirectional manner. To implement server-sent events, developers can use the **EventSource** API in JavaScript to establish an SSE connection and receive server-sent events:

javascriptCopy code

```
var          eventSource          =          new
EventSource('http://example.com/events');
eventSource.onmessage = function(event) { //
Handle incoming server-sent event };
```

Server-sent events are particularly well-suited for scenarios where the server needs to push updates or notifications to clients without requiring client-initiated requests, such as real-time news feeds, live sports updates, or social media notifications.

Push notifications are another important aspect of real-time messaging and notifications, allowing web applications to deliver timely updates and alerts to users even when the application is not actively being used. Push notifications are typically implemented using platform-specific services such as Firebase Cloud Messaging (FCM) for Android devices or Apple Push Notification Service (APNs) for iOS devices. To send push notifications, developers need to integrate their web application with the respective push notification service and obtain the necessary credentials and configuration settings.

For example, to send push notifications to Android devices using Firebase Cloud Messaging (FCM), developers can use the Firebase Admin SDK for Node.js and the **firebase-admin** npm package. After setting up a Firebase project and configuring the necessary credentials, developers can send push notifications to specific devices or topics using the Firebase Admin SDK:

```javascript
javascriptCopy code
const admin = require('firebase-admin');
admin.initializeApp({
  credential: admin.credential.cert('path/to/serviceAccountKey.json'),
});
const message = {
  notification: {
    title: 'New Message',
    body: 'You have a new message!',
  },
  topic: 'news',
};
admin.messaging().send(message)
  .then((response) => {
    console.log('Successfully sent message:', response);
  })
  .catch((error) => {
    console.error('Error sending message:', error);
  });
```

By leveraging push notification services, developers can deliver targeted notifications to users' devices, increasing engagement and keeping users informed about important updates, messages, or events.

In summary, real-time messaging and notifications play a crucial role in enhancing user engagement, facilitating communication, and delivering timely updates in modern web applications. By leveraging technologies such as WebSocket, server-sent events (SSE), and push notifications, developers can implement robust and responsive real-time messaging systems that provide users with seamless communication experiences across various platforms and devices. Whether it's instant messaging, live updates, or push notifications, real-time messaging and notifications empower web applications to deliver dynamic and interactive user experiences in today's fast-paced digital landscape.

Chapter 9: Server-Side Rendering with AJAX

Server-side rendering (SSR) and client-side rendering (CSR) are two fundamental approaches to generating and displaying web content, each with its own advantages and trade-offs. SSR involves rendering web pages on the server and sending fully-formed HTML to the client, while CSR involves rendering web pages dynamically in the client's browser using JavaScript. Understanding the differences between these two rendering strategies is essential for making informed architectural decisions when developing web applications.

In SSR, the server generates HTML content for each page request and sends it to the client, where it is immediately rendered by the browser. This approach is well-suited for applications that prioritize search engine optimization (SEO) and initial page load performance. By delivering pre-rendered HTML to the client, SSR ensures that search engine crawlers can easily index and rank web pages, leading to better discoverability and visibility in search engine results pages (SERPs). Additionally, SSR can improve perceived page load times by delivering meaningful content to users more quickly, especially on devices with slower network connections or limited processing power.

To implement SSR in a web application, developers can use server-side frameworks and libraries such as Next.js for React, Nuxt.js for Vue.js, or Angular Universal for Angular. These frameworks facilitate server-side rendering by pre-rendering React, Vue.js, or Angular components on the server and generating HTML pages dynamically based on incoming requests. By integrating SSR capabilities into their applications, developers can take advantage of the benefits of server-side rendering while still leveraging modern JavaScript frameworks and libraries for building dynamic user interfaces.

On the other hand, CSR involves rendering web pages dynamically in the client's browser using JavaScript, typically in response to user interactions or navigation events. With CSR, the server sends minimal HTML markup and JavaScript code to the client, allowing the browser to fetch additional data and render the page's content dynamically. This approach offers greater flexibility and interactivity, enabling rich, interactive user experiences with seamless transitions and real-time updates. Additionally, CSR is well-suited for applications that require frequent data updates or complex user interactions, such as single-page applications (SPAs) or progressive web apps (PWAs).

To implement CSR in a web application, developers can use modern JavaScript frameworks and libraries such as React, Vue.js, or Angular, which provide robust client-side rendering capabilities out of the box. These frameworks allow developers to build dynamic, interactive user interfaces with ease, leveraging features such as virtual DOM reconciliation, component-based architecture, and state management. By offloading rendering logic to the client, CSR enables applications to deliver fast, responsive user experiences without the need for full-page reloads or server round-trips.

While SSR and CSR offer distinct advantages and trade-offs, it's essential to choose the rendering approach that best aligns with the requirements and constraints of your web application. For content-heavy websites or applications that prioritize SEO and initial page load performance, SSR may be the preferred choice. Conversely, for interactive, data-driven applications with complex user interactions, CSR may offer greater flexibility and responsiveness. In some cases, a hybrid approach combining SSR and CSR, known as "isomorphic" or "universal" rendering, may provide the best of both worlds, allowing developers to leverage the benefits of both server-side and client-side rendering techniques.

In summary, server-side rendering (SSR) and client-side rendering (CSR) are two complementary approaches to generating and displaying web content, each with its own strengths and weaknesses. SSR prioritizes search engine optimization (SEO) and initial page load performance by rendering pages on the server and sending fully-formed HTML to the client. On the other hand, CSR offers greater flexibility and interactivity by rendering pages dynamically in the client's browser using JavaScript. By understanding the differences between these two rendering strategies, developers can make informed architectural decisions when designing and implementing web applications, choosing the approach that best aligns with their application's requirements and objectives.

Integrating server-side rendering (SSR) with AJAX (Asynchronous JavaScript and XML) is a technique employed to enhance the performance and user experience of web applications by combining the benefits of both approaches. Server-side rendering involves generating the HTML content of a web page on the server and sending the pre-rendered HTML to the client, while AJAX enables asynchronous data exchange between the client and server without requiring a full page reload. By integrating SSR with AJAX, developers can achieve the best of both worlds: the initial fast load times and search engine optimization (SEO) benefits of SSR, coupled with the dynamic and interactive nature of AJAX-driven client-side updates.

To integrate server-side rendering with AJAX, developers typically utilize frameworks or libraries that support SSR, such as Next.js for React applications or Nuxt.js for Vue.js applications. These frameworks provide built-in support for SSR and offer features that streamline the integration of AJAX functionality.

One common scenario where integrating SSR with AJAX is beneficial is in applications that require dynamic data fetching after the initial page load. For example, consider an e-commerce website where product listings need to be fetched from a server-side API and displayed on the client-side. By leveraging SSR, developers can pre-render the initial product listings on the server and send them to the client as part of the initial HTML response, ensuring fast page load times and improved SEO.

Once the initial page is loaded, AJAX can be used to fetch additional data, such as product details, user reviews, or shopping cart information, without requiring a full page reload. This asynchronous data fetching allows for a seamless user experience, where users can interact with the application without experiencing delays or interruptions.

To implement SSR with AJAX using Next.js, developers can follow these steps:

Install Next.js in your project using npm or yarn:

luaCopy code

```
npm install next react react-dom
```

Create a new Next.js page component that will handle server-side rendering and AJAX data fetching. For example, you can create a file named **products.js** in the **pages** directory:

jsxCopy code

```
// pages/products.js import { useEffect, useState }
from 'react'; const ProductsPage = () => { const
```

```
[products, setProducts] = useState([]); useEffect((()
=> { const fetchProducts = async () => { const
response = await fetch('/api/products'); const data
= await response.json(); setProducts(data); };
fetchProducts(); }, []); return ( <div>
<h1>Products</h1> <ul> {products.map((product) =>
( <li key={product.id}>{product.name}</li> ))} </ul>
</div> ); }; export default ProductsPage;
```

Define an API route to handle the AJAX data fetching on the server-side. Create a file named **products.js** in the **pages/api** directory:

javascriptCopy code

```
// pages/api/products.js const products = [ { id: 1,
name: 'Product 1' }, { id: 2, name: 'Product 2' }, {
id: 3, name: 'Product 3' }, ]; export default function
handler(req, res) { res.status(200).json(products); }
```

Start the Next.js development server:

luaCopy code

```
npx next dev
```

With these steps, you have integrated server-side rendering with AJAX in a Next.js application. When a user navigates to the **/products** page, Next.js will pre-render the page on the server and send the initial HTML response with the product listings. Subsequently, AJAX will be used to fetch additional product data from the server-side API without requiring a full page reload.

Integrating SSR with AJAX offers several benefits, including improved performance, SEO optimization, and a seamless user experience. By leveraging the strengths of both approaches, developers can build fast, dynamic, and interactive web applications that meet the demands of modern users.

Chapter 10: Handling Large Data Sets in AJAX Applications

Efficient data pagination techniques play a crucial role in optimizing the performance and user experience of web applications, especially those dealing with large datasets. Pagination refers to the process of dividing content into discrete pages, allowing users to navigate through the data in manageable chunks. By implementing efficient pagination techniques, developers can minimize loading times, reduce server load, and enhance usability.

One common pagination technique is the "Limit-Offset" method, which involves retrieving a specified number of records (limit) starting from a particular offset position. This approach is widely used in database queries and API endpoints to fetch paginated data. For example, in SQL databases, the LIMIT and OFFSET clauses are often employed to limit the number of rows returned by a query:

sqlCopy code

```
SELECT * FROM products LIMIT 10 OFFSET 20;
```

In this query, the database retrieves 10 records starting from the 21st record (offset 20).

Another pagination technique is "Keyset Pagination," also known as "Cursor Pagination" or "Pagination by Continuation Token." Unlike the Limit-Offset method, Keyset Pagination relies on unique identifiers (keys) to paginate through the dataset. Instead of using offsets, it uses the last retrieved key to fetch the next set of records. This technique is particularly useful for datasets where the order of records is important and may change over time.

For example, in an e-commerce application, Keyset Pagination can be used to paginate through product listings based on their IDs:

sqlCopy code

```
SELECT * FROM products WHERE id > last_id ORDER BY id ASC LIMIT 10;
```

Here, **last_id** represents the ID of the last retrieved record, and the query fetches the next 10 records with IDs greater than **last_id**.

In addition to database-level pagination, client-side pagination techniques can also be employed to further optimize performance and reduce server load. With client-side pagination, the entire dataset is loaded into the client's browser, and pagination is handled locally without requiring additional server requests. This approach is suitable for small to medium-sized datasets that can be comfortably loaded and processed on the client-side.

Frameworks and libraries such as React, Angular, and Vue.js offer built-in support for client-side pagination, allowing developers to implement pagination components and logic easily. For example, in a React application, developers can create a pagination component that manages pagination state and

renders pagination controls based on the total number of pages and the current page:
jsxCopy code

```jsx
import React from 'react'; const Pagination = ({ currentPage, totalPages, onPageChange }) => { const handlePrevPage = () => { onPageChange(currentPage - 1); }; const handleNextPage = () => { onPageChange(currentPage + 1); }; return ( <div> <button onClick={handlePrevPage} disabled={currentPage === 1}>Previous</button> <span>{currentPage} / {totalPages}</span> <button onClick={handleNextPage} disabled={currentPage === totalPages}>Next</button> </div> ); }; export default Pagination;
```

With this Pagination component, developers can easily implement client-side pagination in their React applications by managing the current page state and updating it based on user interactions.

Furthermore, developers can combine server-side and client-side pagination techniques to achieve optimal performance and scalability. For instance, they can use server-side pagination to fetch large datasets efficiently while employing client-side pagination for smoother navigation and enhanced user experience.

In summary, efficient data pagination techniques are essential for optimizing the performance and usability of web applications handling large datasets. By leveraging both server-side and client-side pagination methods, developers can strike a balance between server load, network latency, and user experience, ensuring that users can navigate through data seamlessly and efficiently.

Lazy loading and virtualization are indispensable techniques for managing large datasets in web applications. With the exponential growth of data in modern web environments, handling vast amounts of information efficiently has become a significant challenge. Lazy loading and virtualization offer solutions to this problem by optimizing resource usage and enhancing user experience.

Lazy loading, also known as "on-demand loading," is a strategy that defers the loading of non-essential resources until they are needed. This approach is particularly beneficial when dealing with large datasets, as it allows web applications to load only the portion of data that is currently visible to the user, reducing initial load times and conserving memory resources.

One common implementation of lazy loading involves loading data as the user scrolls through a page. As the user reaches the end of the currently loaded content, additional data is fetched from the server and appended to the page dynamically, ensuring a smooth and uninterrupted browsing experience.

In JavaScript frameworks like React or Angular, lazy loading can be achieved using libraries such as React.lazy() or Angular's loadChildren() function. These features allow developers to asynchronously load components or modules only when they are needed, minimizing the initial bundle size and improving application performance.

For example, in React, lazy loading a component can be done as follows:

jsxCopy code

```
const LazyComponent = React.lazy(() => import('./LazyComponent'));
```

This code asynchronously imports the 'LazyComponent' module, ensuring that it is loaded only when it is rendered on the screen.

Virtualization, on the other hand, involves rendering only the visible portion of a large dataset, rather than rendering the entire dataset at once. This technique is particularly useful for scenarios where loading the entire dataset into memory would be impractical or resource-intensive.

Virtualized lists and grids are common implementations of this technique. Instead of rendering all items in a list or grid simultaneously, only the items that are currently visible within the viewport are rendered. As the user scrolls, new items are dynamically rendered while off-screen items are recycled or removed from the DOM, resulting in improved performance and reduced memory usage.

Frameworks like React offer libraries such as react-virtualized or react-window for implementing virtualized lists and grids. These libraries efficiently manage the rendering of large datasets by dynamically rendering only the visible items, thus optimizing performance even with extremely large datasets.

For instance, using react-window, developers can create a virtualized list component as follows:

jsxCopy code

import { FixedSizeList } from 'react-window'; const VirtualizedList = ({ data }) => (<FixedSizeList height={400} width={300} itemSize={50} itemCount={data.length} > {(({ index, style }) => (<div style={style}>{data[index]}</div>)} </FixedSizeList>);

In this example, the FixedSizeList component from react-window efficiently renders a virtualized list of items, ensuring optimal performance even with a large dataset.

By combining lazy loading and virtualization techniques, developers can create web applications that efficiently handle large datasets while maintaining a responsive and seamless user experience. These techniques are essential tools in the developer's arsenal for building high-performance web applications capable of handling the challenges posed by modern data-intensive environments.

BOOK 4
MASTERING AJAX
ARCHITECTING ROBUST WEB AND MOBILE SOLUTIONS

ROB BOTWRIGHT

Chapter 1: Architectural Principles in AJAX Development

Separation of concerns is a fundamental principle in software engineering that advocates for dividing a computer program into distinct sections, each addressing a specific concern or responsibility. When applied to AJAX architecture, this principle plays a crucial role in designing scalable, maintainable, and efficient web applications.

At its core, separation of concerns in AJAX architecture involves dividing the various aspects of application development – such as presentation, business logic, and data management – into separate modules or layers. This separation allows developers to focus on specific tasks without having to worry about the complexities of other components, resulting in cleaner code, easier maintenance, and better scalability.

One of the primary areas where separation of concerns is evident in AJAX architecture is in the division between client-side and server-side code. AJAX, which stands for Asynchronous JavaScript and XML, enables the development of dynamic web applications by allowing asynchronous communication between the client and server. This separation allows for a more responsive user experience, as data can be retrieved and updated without requiring a full page reload.

On the client side, separation of concerns is achieved through the use of JavaScript frameworks and libraries, such as React, Angular, or Vue.js. These frameworks provide tools for structuring client-side code in a modular and organized manner, often following the Model-View-Controller (MVC) or Model-View-ViewModel (MVVM) architectural patterns.

For example, in a React application, components are used to encapsulate UI elements and associated behavior, promoting a clear separation between presentation and logic. Each component is responsible for rendering a specific part of the user interface and handling user interactions, making it easier to understand and maintain the codebase.

bashCopy code

```
npm install react
```

In the server-side code, separation of concerns is achieved through the use of server-side technologies such as Node.js, Python Django, or Ruby on Rails. These frameworks provide tools for organizing server-side code into modules, routing requests, and interacting with databases. By separating the concerns of handling HTTP requests, business logic, and data persistence, developers can build scalable and maintainable server-side applications.

bashCopy code

```
npm install express
```

Another aspect of separation of concerns in AJAX architecture is the division between data retrieval and presentation. In traditional web applications, data retrieval and presentation logic are often tightly coupled, making it difficult to modify one without affecting the other. However, with AJAX, data retrieval can be decoupled from the presentation layer, allowing for greater flexibility and reusability.

javascriptCopy code

```
// Example AJAX request using Fetch API
fetch('/api/data') .then(response => response.json()) .then(data => { // Handle retrieved data }) .catch(error => { // Handle errors });
```

By using AJAX to asynchronously fetch data from the server, developers can separate the concerns of data retrieval and presentation, making it easier to update the user interface without affecting the underlying data model. This approach also enables developers to build more responsive and interactive web applications, as data can be updated dynamically without requiring a full page reload.

In summary, separation of concerns is a fundamental principle in AJAX architecture that promotes modularization, maintainability, and scalability. By dividing the various aspects of application development into separate modules or layers, developers can build web applications that are easier to understand, modify, and extend. Whether it's separating client-side and server-side code, or decoupling data retrieval from presentation logic, separation of concerns plays a crucial role in building robust and efficient AJAX applications.

Modular design patterns are essential for building scalable and maintainable AJAX applications. These patterns provide a structured approach to organizing code, promoting reusability, flexibility, and separation of concerns. By breaking down complex systems into smaller, self-contained modules, developers can create more manageable and robust applications.

One widely used modular design pattern in AJAX development is the Module Pattern. This pattern encapsulates functionality within individual modules, allowing for better organization and encapsulation of code. Modules can be created using functions or objects, with private and public methods to control access to internal functionality.

To illustrate, consider an AJAX application that retrieves data from an API and displays it on a web page. Using the Module Pattern, you can create separate modules for handling data retrieval, UI rendering, and event handling.

```
javascriptCopy code
// Module for data retrieval var dataModule =
(function() { // Private variables and functions var
apiUrl = 'https://api.example.com/data'; // Public
methods return { fetchData: function(callback) { //
Make AJAX request to fetch data // Example
```

command: fetch(apiUrl) // Handle response and invoke callback } }; })(); // Module for UI rendering var uiModule = (function() { // Private variables and functions var renderData = function(data) { // Render data on the UI }; // Public methods return { displayData: function(data) { // Example command: renderData(data) // Display data on the UI } }; })(); // Module for event handling var eventModule = (function(dataModule, uiModule) { // Private variables and functions var handleButtonClick = function() { // Example event listener command: document.getElementById('button').addEventListener ('click', function() {...}); // When button is clicked, fetch data and display it dataModule.fetchData(uiModule.displayData); }; // Public methods return { init: function() { // Example command: handleButtonClick() // Initialize event handlers } }; })(dataModule, uiModule); // Initialize the application eventModule.init();

In this example, the dataModule handles data retrieval using AJAX, the uiModule is responsible for rendering data on the UI, and the eventModule manages event handling. Each module operates independently and can be tested, modified, and reused without affecting other parts of the application.

Another modular design pattern commonly used in AJAX applications is the Revealing Module Pattern.

This pattern is similar to the Module Pattern but exposes only the necessary functions and variables, keeping the rest private.

javascriptCopy code

```
var module = (function() { // Private variables and functions var privateVar = 'private'; var privateFunction = function() { // Private function logic }; // Public variables and functions return { publicVar: 'public', publicFunction: function() { // Public function logic } }; })();
```

The Revealing Module Pattern allows developers to create cleaner and more readable code by explicitly declaring which variables and functions are publicly accessible.

Additionally, the Observer Pattern is commonly used in AJAX applications to implement event-driven communication between modules. This pattern allows modules to subscribe to and receive notifications about changes or events without being tightly coupled.

javascriptCopy code

```
// Subject module var subject = (function() { var observers = []; return { addObserver: function(observer) { observers.push(observer); }, notifyObservers: function(data) { observers.forEach(function(observer) { observer.update(data); }); } }; })(); // Observer module var observer = { update: function(data) { //
```

Handle update } }; // Register observer subject. addObserver (observer);

By implementing modular design patterns such as the Module Pattern, Revealing Module Pattern, and Observer Pattern, developers can create more maintainable, scalable, and flexible AJAX applications. These patterns promote code organization, encapsulation, and decoupling, leading to improved code quality and developer productivity.

Chapter 2: Scalable Data Management Strategies

Data normalization is a crucial aspect of AJAX development, aiming to organize data efficiently for storage and retrieval while minimizing redundancy and improving data integrity. By employing various normalization techniques, developers can streamline data management, enhance application performance, and ensure consistency across the system.

One common data normalization technique is the process of breaking down complex data structures into smaller, atomic units. This approach, known as First Normal Form (1NF), involves eliminating repeating groups and ensuring that each attribute contains only atomic values. By adhering to 1NF, developers can avoid data duplication and simplify data manipulation operations.

To illustrate, consider a scenario where an e-commerce application stores product information in a single table. Instead of storing multiple attributes in a single field (e.g., product details), developers can decompose the data into separate fields such as product name, description, price, and category. This restructuring facilitates efficient querying and manipulation of product data.

Another level of data normalization involves adhering to Second Normal Form (2NF), which builds upon 1NF by addressing partial dependencies within the dataset. In 2NF, each non-key attribute is functionally dependent on the entire primary key, eliminating redundancy and ensuring that all data is logically related.

For instance, imagine an inventory management system where product data is stored in a table with attributes such as product ID, product name, supplier ID, and supplier name. To achieve 2NF, developers can separate the supplier information into a separate table, establishing a one-to-many relationship between products and suppliers based on their respective IDs.

Beyond 2NF, Third Normal Form (3NF) further refines data normalization by removing transitive dependencies between attributes. In 3NF, every non-key attribute is directly dependent on the primary key, and no transitive dependencies exist between non-key attributes.

Continuing with the previous example, suppose the product table includes an attribute for supplier contact information, such as supplier email. If the supplier email is functionally dependent on the supplier name rather than the primary key (supplier ID), it creates a transitive dependency. By extracting the supplier contact details into a separate table linked by the supplier ID, developers can achieve 3NF and eliminate transitive dependencies.

While adhering to traditional normalization techniques like 1NF, 2NF, and 3NF is essential for database design, AJAX applications often require additional considerations due to their dynamic and asynchronous nature. One such consideration is denormalization, a technique that deliberately introduces redundancy to optimize query performance and improve data accessibility.

In AJAX applications, denormalization can be beneficial for frequently accessed data that requires rapid retrieval. For example, a social media platform may denormalize user profile data by duplicating certain attributes (e.g., username, profile picture) across multiple tables to minimize joins and enhance responsiveness when fetching user information.

Furthermore, developers can leverage caching mechanisms to improve the performance of AJAX applications by storing frequently accessed data in memory or on disk. By caching AJAX responses, developers can reduce server load, minimize latency, and enhance user experience.

To implement caching in an AJAX application, developers can utilize frameworks or libraries that offer built-in caching features, such as Redis or Memcached. Additionally, developers can employ browser caching by setting appropriate HTTP headers to instruct browsers to store AJAX responses locally.

In summary, data normalization is a fundamental aspect of AJAX development, enabling developers to organize data efficiently, minimize redundancy, and ensure data integrity. By adhering to normalization principles such as 1NF, 2NF, and 3NF, developers can create robust database schemas that support reliable data storage and retrieval. Additionally, techniques like denormalization and caching play a crucial role in optimizing the performance of AJAX applications, enhancing responsiveness, and improving user experience.

Data sharding is a crucial technique for achieving scalability in modern database systems. It involves horizontally partitioning data across multiple database instances, enabling distributed storage and parallel processing of data. By distributing data shards across multiple servers or nodes, organizations can handle larger volumes of data and support increased application traffic without sacrificing performance or reliability.

One of the primary motivations for implementing data sharding is to address the limitations of traditional monolithic database architectures, which often struggle to scale effectively as data volumes grow. In a monolithic architecture, a single database server is responsible for storing and managing all data, leading to performance bottlenecks and scalability challenges as the dataset expands. By contrast, data sharding distributes the data workload across multiple database instances, allowing organizations to scale horizontally by adding more servers or nodes to the system.

To illustrate the concept of data sharding, consider an e-commerce platform that stores customer order data in a relational database. In a monolithic setup, all order records would reside on a single database server, potentially leading to performance issues during peak traffic periods or as the number of orders increases over time. By implementing data sharding, the platform can partition the order data across multiple database shards based on a predefined sharding key, such as customer ID or order date. Each shard is hosted on a separate database server, enabling parallel processing of orders and improved scalability.

There are several approaches to implementing data sharding, each with its own benefits and trade-offs. One common technique is range-based sharding, where data is partitioned based on a predetermined range of values. For example, in a range-based sharding scheme, customer orders could be partitioned based on the order date, with each shard responsible for storing orders within a specific date range. Range-based sharding is relatively straightforward to implement and can be effective for workloads with evenly distributed data.

Another approach to data sharding is hash-based sharding, where data is partitioned based on a hash function applied to a sharding key. In a hash-based sharding scheme, the sharding key (e.g., customer ID) is hashed to generate a numeric value, which is then used to determine the target shard for storing the data. Hash-based sharding can provide better data distribution and load balancing compared to range-based sharding, especially for workloads with skewed data distributions.

In addition to range-based and hash-based sharding, organizations can also implement composite sharding strategies that combine multiple sharding techniques to achieve optimal performance and scalability. For example, a hybrid sharding approach might use range-based sharding for some data partitions and hash-based sharding for others, depending on the characteristics of the dataset and workload.

Once the data sharding strategy is defined, organizations must implement the necessary infrastructure and tools to support distributed data storage and processing. This typically involves deploying a distributed database system that supports sharding, such as MongoDB, Cassandra, or Amazon DynamoDB. These databases provide built-in support for sharding, allowing organizations to configure and manage shard clusters with ease.

To deploy a sharded database cluster using MongoDB, for example, organizations can use the MongoDB Atlas cloud service, which offers a fully managed database solution with built-in support for sharding. With MongoDB Atlas, organizations can create a sharded cluster with just a few clicks, configure sharding keys, and scale the cluster as needed to accommodate growing data volumes and traffic.

In addition to deploying the database infrastructure, organizations must also modify their application code to support data sharding. This may involve updating data access logic to ensure that queries are routed to the appropriate shard based on the sharding key. Application frameworks and libraries can simplify this process by providing abstractions for sharded database access and transparent routing of queries to the correct shard.

Once the sharded database cluster is deployed and the application code is updated, organizations can benefit from improved scalability, performance, and reliability. By distributing data across multiple shards, organizations can handle larger workloads and support more users without experiencing performance degradation or downtime. Additionally, data sharding provides fault tolerance and high availability, as each shard can be replicated across multiple nodes to ensure data durability and resilience.

In summary, data sharding is a powerful technique for achieving scalability in modern database systems. By horizontally partitioning data across multiple database instances, organizations can handle larger volumes of data and support increased application traffic without sacrificing performance or reliability. By implementing the necessary infrastructure and tools, organizations can deploy sharded database clusters and update their application code to support data sharding, enabling them to scale their applications effectively and meet the demands of a growing user base.

Chapter 3: Advanced AJAX Routing Techniques

Dynamic route handling is a crucial aspect of building modern AJAX applications, enabling developers to create dynamic, interactive web experiences where content changes dynamically based on user interactions or data updates. By implementing dynamic route handling, developers can efficiently manage navigation, load content dynamically, and provide seamless user experiences.

One of the primary benefits of dynamic route handling is its ability to enable single-page application (SPA) behavior, where navigation between different sections or views of the application occurs without a full page reload. Instead, the application dynamically updates the content of the current page based on the requested route or URL.

In JavaScript frameworks like React, Vue.js, or Angular, dynamic route handling is typically achieved using routing libraries or built-in routing features. For example, in React applications, developers can use the React Router library to define route configurations and render components based on the current URL. To install React Router using npm, developers can use the following command:

Copy code

npm install react-router-dom

Once installed, developers can define route configurations using the **<Route>** component provided by React Router and specify the corresponding component to render for each route. Additionally, developers can use features like nested routes, route parameters, and route guards to implement more complex routing logic.

In Vue.js applications, developers can achieve dynamic route handling using the Vue Router library, which provides similar functionality to React Router. To install Vue Router using npm, developers can use the following command:

Copy code

npm install vue-router

After installation, developers can define route configurations using the **VueRouter** instance and specify route components using the **component** option. Vue Router also supports features like nested routes, route parameters, and navigation guards to handle authentication, authorization, and other route-related tasks.

In addition to client-side routing, dynamic route handling in AJAX applications often involves server-side routing to handle API requests and serve dynamic content. In Node.js applications, developers can use frameworks like Express.js to define server-side routes and handle incoming requests. To create a new Express.js application, developers can use the following command:

cssCopy code

npm install express --save

Once installed, developers can define route handlers for different endpoints using the Express Router and specify the corresponding logic to handle each request. For example, to define a route that fetches user data from a database and returns it as JSON, developers can use the following code:

javascriptCopy code

```
const express = require('express'); const app = express(); // Define a route handler for GET /users app.get('/users', (req, res) => { // Fetch user data from the database const users = [...]; // Fetch users from the database // Send the user data as JSON res.json(users); }); // Start the Express server app.listen(3000, () => { console.log('Server is running on port 3000'); });
```

By implementing dynamic route handling on both the client and server sides, developers can create AJAX applications that offer seamless navigation, efficient content loading, and enhanced user experiences. Whether building SPAs, progressive web apps (PWAs), or hybrid mobile applications, dynamic route handling remains a fundamental aspect of modern web development, enabling developers to build rich, interactive web experiences that respond to user actions in real-time.

Route guards and resolvers play a critical role in AJAX routing, ensuring that navigation within an application occurs smoothly and securely. These mechanisms provide developers with the ability to control access to certain routes, fetch necessary data before rendering components, and handle asynchronous operations seamlessly.

In frameworks like Angular, route guards are used to protect routes based on certain conditions, such as user authentication status or permissions. These guards can prevent unauthorized access to certain parts of an application, redirect users to login pages if they are not authenticated, or restrict access based on user roles. To create a route guard in an Angular application, developers can use the Angular CLI to generate a guard file:

bashCopy code

ng generate guard auth

This command creates an **auth.guard.ts** file, which contains a class implementing the **CanActivate** interface. Inside the **canActivate** method, developers can implement the logic to check whether a user is authenticated and return a boolean value accordingly. If the user is authenticated, the method returns **true**, allowing access to the route; otherwise, it returns **false**, preventing access.

Route resolvers, on the other hand, are used to fetch data before navigating to a route's component. This ensures that the necessary data is available when rendering the component, preventing empty or incomplete views. Resolvers are especially useful when dealing with asynchronous data fetching operations, such as HTTP requests to fetch data from a server.

In Angular, developers can create a resolver using the Angular CLI:

bashCopy code

ng generate resolver data

This command generates a **data.resolver.ts** file, which contains a class implementing the **Resolve** interface. Inside the **resolve** method, developers can implement the logic to fetch data asynchronously. Once the data is fetched successfully, the resolver returns an observable or promise containing the resolved data, which Angular uses to render the component.

Route guards and resolvers work together seamlessly to enhance the routing experience in AJAX applications. For example, a route guard can be used to ensure that only authenticated users can access certain routes, while a resolver fetches necessary data before rendering the component. Combined, these mechanisms provide a robust solution for managing navigation and data fetching in AJAX applications.

In addition to Angular, other frameworks like React and Vue.js also provide similar capabilities for implementing route guards and resolvers. In React, developers can use libraries like React Router to define route guards and implement data fetching logic using component lifecycle methods or custom hooks. Similarly, Vue.js provides built-in navigation guards and supports asynchronous route resolution using **beforeRouteEnter** and **beforeRouteUpdate** hooks.

By leveraging route guards and resolvers, developers can build AJAX applications that offer enhanced security, data consistency, and user experience. Whether building single-page applications, progressive web apps, or complex enterprise solutions, these techniques play a crucial role in ensuring that routes are protected, data is fetched efficiently, and users have a seamless navigation experience.

Chapter 4: Responsive Design for AJAX Applications

Media queries and breakpoints are fundamental tools in responsive web design, including AJAX-based applications. They allow developers to create layouts that adapt to different screen sizes and devices, providing a consistent user experience across various platforms. Understanding how to use media queries effectively is essential for building modern web applications that cater to a diverse range of devices and screen sizes.

In CSS, media queries are used to apply styles based on characteristics of the user's device, such as screen width, height, orientation, and resolution. By defining different sets of styles for specific conditions, developers can create layouts that adjust dynamically to accommodate different viewport sizes.

To define a media query in CSS, developers use the **@media** rule followed by one or more media features and conditions. For example, to apply styles when the viewport width is less than or equal to 768 pixels, developers can write:

cssCopy code

```
@media (max-width: 768px) { /* Styles for screens less than or equal to 768px wide */ }
```

Similarly, breakpoints are specific points in the CSS where the layout of the web page changes to accommodate different screen sizes. Breakpoints are typically defined using media queries and correspond to common device widths, such as smartphones, tablets, laptops, and desktops.

When designing an AJAX-based application, developers should consider how media queries and breakpoints affect the user experience. By designing responsive layouts that adapt to various screen sizes, developers can ensure that users have a consistent and optimal experience regardless of the device they are using.

One common approach to using media queries and breakpoints in AJAX applications is to create a mobile-first design. This means starting with the styles for smaller screens and then using media queries to add additional styles for larger screens. This approach ensures that the application is optimized for mobile devices by default and progressively enhances the layout for larger screens.

In addition to screen size, media queries can also target other device characteristics, such as orientation (portrait or landscape) and resolution (high or low dpi). This allows developers to create highly tailored layouts that adapt not only to different screen sizes but also to other device-specific attributes.

For example, developers can use media queries to apply specific styles when the device is in landscape mode:

cssCopy code

```css
@media (orientation: landscape) { /* Styles for landscape orientation */ }
```

Or they can target devices with high-resolution displays:

cssCopy code

```
@media (min-resolution: 2dppx) { /* Styles for high-resolution displays */ }
```

By combining media queries with breakpoints, developers can create flexible and adaptive layouts that provide an optimal viewing experience across a wide range of devices and screen sizes. This approach is essential for ensuring that AJAX applications are accessible and user-friendly on smartphones, tablets, laptops, desktops, and other devices.

Furthermore, modern CSS frameworks like Bootstrap and Foundation provide built-in support for responsive design, including predefined breakpoints and utility classes for hiding or showing elements based on screen size. These frameworks simplify the process of creating responsive layouts and allow developers to focus on building robust AJAX functionality without worrying about the intricacies of CSS media queries.

In summary, media queries and breakpoints are essential tools for creating responsive and adaptive layouts in AJAX-based applications. By using media queries to define different styles for specific device characteristics and breakpoints to adjust the layout at key screen sizes, developers can ensure that their applications look and perform optimally across a wide range of devices and screen resolutions. Whether building a simple web application or a complex enterprise solution, mastering the use of media queries and breakpoints is crucial for delivering a seamless user experience in today's multi-device world.

Flexbox and Grid Layouts are powerful tools in modern web development, offering flexible and efficient ways to create responsive layouts in AJAX-based applications. These layout systems provide developers with fine-grained control over the positioning and alignment of elements, allowing them to design interfaces that adapt seamlessly to different screen sizes and orientations. Understanding how to leverage Flexbox and Grid Layouts is essential for building modern web applications that deliver a consistent user experience across a wide range of devices and viewports.

Flexbox, short for Flexible Box Layout, is a one-dimensional layout model that excels at aligning items within a container along a single axis, either horizontally or vertically. It provides a straightforward way to distribute space among items in a container, making it ideal for building dynamic and responsive layouts. Flexbox is especially useful for creating navigation menus, card-based layouts, and other components where the arrangement of items may change based on available space.

To use Flexbox in CSS, developers apply the **display: flex** property to a container element, which turns it into a flex container. They can then use various properties like **justify-content**, **align-items**, and **flex** to control the alignment, distribution, and sizing of items within the container.

For example, to create a horizontal navigation menu where the items are evenly spaced and centered, developers can use the following CSS:

cssCopy code

.nav-menu { display: flex; justify-content: space-around; align-items: center; }

Grid Layout, on the other hand, is a two-dimensional layout system that allows developers to create complex grid-based designs with rows and columns. It provides precise control over the placement of elements within a grid, making it ideal for building responsive grid layouts, such as those commonly found in e-commerce websites, dashboards, and data-intensive applications.

To use Grid Layout in CSS, developers define a grid container by applying the **display: grid** property to a parent element. They can then define the structure of the grid using properties like **grid-template-columns** and **grid-template-rows**, specifying the size and alignment of columns and rows.

For example, to create a simple grid layout with three columns of equal width, developers can use the following CSS:

cssCopy code

.grid-container { display: grid; grid-template-columns: repeat(3, 1fr); gap: 20px; /* Optional gap between grid items */ }

Both Flexbox and Grid Layout offer powerful features for building responsive designs, and developers often use them in combination to achieve more complex layouts. For example, developers may use Flexbox to align items within a grid item or use Grid Layout to create a flexible grid container with dynamic column and row sizing.

In the context of AJAX-based applications, Flexbox and Grid Layouts play a crucial role in creating responsive user interfaces that adapt to different screen sizes and orientations. Whether building a simple blog or a sophisticated web application, developers can leverage these layout systems to create visually appealing and user-friendly interfaces that provide a seamless experience across devices.

When designing AJAX-based applications with Flexbox and Grid Layouts, developers should consider the following best practices:

Mobile-first Design: Start by designing layouts for small screens and then use media queries to progressively enhance the layout for larger screens. This approach ensures that the application is optimized for mobile devices by default.

Use Flexbox for Simple Layouts: Flexbox is well-suited for simple layouts where items need to be aligned along a single axis. Use Flexbox for components like navigation menus, card grids, and flexible layouts.

Leverage Grid Layout for Complex Grids: Grid Layout is ideal for creating complex grid-based designs with multiple rows and columns. Use Grid Layout for components like data tables, dashboards, and multi-column layouts.

Combine Flexbox and Grid for Advanced Layouts: For more complex layouts, consider using Flexbox and Grid Layout together to achieve precise control over the arrangement and alignment of elements within a container.

Test Across Devices and Viewports: Always test the application across various devices and viewports to ensure that the layout looks and behaves as expected on different screen sizes and orientations.

By following these best practices and mastering the use of Flexbox and Grid Layouts, developers can create modern and responsive AJAX-based applications that provide an optimal user experience across devices and platforms. Whether building a small website or a large-scale web application, Flexbox and Grid Layouts offer powerful tools for designing flexible and adaptive layouts that meet the needs of today's diverse user base.

Chapter 5: Integrating AJAX with Progressive Web Apps (PWA)

Progressive Web Applications (PWAs) represent a modern approach to building web applications that offer users an experience similar to native mobile apps. The architecture of PWAs combines the best features of web and mobile app development, leveraging web technologies to deliver fast, reliable, and engaging user experiences across devices and platforms.

At the core of PWA architecture is the concept of progressive enhancement, which allows developers to start with a basic web application and progressively add more advanced features and capabilities as the user's browser and device support them. This approach ensures that PWAs are accessible to all users regardless of their device or browser capabilities, while still providing advanced features to users with modern browsers and devices.

The architecture of a PWA typically consists of several key components, including:

Service Worker: Service workers are the heart of PWA architecture, enabling features such as offline support, background synchronization, and push notifications. A service worker is a JavaScript file that runs in the background separate from the main browser thread, allowing it to intercept and handle network requests, cache assets, and perform other tasks asynchronously. To register a service worker in a PWA, developers use the **navigator.serviceWorker.register()** method in the JavaScript code of their application.

App Shell: The app shell is the minimal HTML, CSS, and JavaScript required to render the user interface of the application. It serves as the foundation of the PWA and is typically cached by the service worker to ensure fast loading times and offline accessibility. The app shell is responsible for providing the basic structure and layout of the application, while the content is dynamically loaded and updated using data from the server or local cache.

Web App Manifest: The web app manifest is a JSON file that provides metadata about the PWA, such as its name, description, icon, and theme colors. The manifest allows users to add the PWA to their home screen and launch it like a native app. To create a web app manifest, developers include a **<link>** element in the HTML code of their application and specify the path to the manifest file.

Responsive Design: Responsive design is essential for PWAs to ensure that the user interface adapts seamlessly to different screen sizes and orientations. Developers use CSS media queries and flexible layout techniques to create responsive layouts that look great on desktops, tablets, and smartphones. Responsive design is particularly important for PWAs because they are intended to work across a wide range of devices and form factors.

Progressive Enhancement: Progressive enhancement is a fundamental principle of PWA architecture, enabling developers to build applications that work for all users regardless of their device or browser capabilities. By starting with a basic HTML-based interface and adding advanced features and capabilities using modern web technologies like service workers and web APIs, developers can ensure that their PWAs are accessible to as many users as possible.

Network Strategies: PWAs employ various network strategies to optimize performance and reliability, especially in challenging network conditions. These strategies include caching static assets for offline access, pre-caching resources for faster load times, and using adaptive loading techniques to prioritize critical content. Developers can configure the behavior of the service worker to implement these network strategies based on factors like network connectivity and resource availability.

Security Considerations: Security is a critical aspect of PWA architecture, especially when handling sensitive user data or performing transactions. Developers must follow best practices for securing their applications, such as using HTTPS to encrypt data in transit, implementing proper authentication and authorization mechanisms, and validating user input to prevent common security vulnerabilities like cross-site scripting (XSS) and cross-site request forgery (CSRF).

Cross-Browser Compatibility: Ensuring cross-browser compatibility is essential for PWAs to reach a broad audience of users across different web browsers and platforms. Developers must thoroughly test their applications on various browsers and devices to identify and address compatibility issues, ensuring that the PWA delivers a consistent and reliable experience for all users.

Overall, the architecture of PWAs is designed to leverage the capabilities of modern web browsers and devices to deliver fast, reliable, and engaging user experiences. By combining progressive enhancement, responsive design, network optimization, and security best practices, developers can create PWAs that provide users with a native-like experience while retaining the reach and accessibility of the web.

Implementing Service Workers for offline support in AJAX applications is a crucial aspect of modern web development, enabling users to access content even when they're offline or experiencing poor network conditions. Service workers are JavaScript files that run in the background of a web application, providing features like caching, network interception, and push notifications. By leveraging service workers, developers can enhance the reliability and performance of their AJAX applications, ensuring a seamless user experience across different devices and network environments.

To implement Service Workers for offline support in AJAX applications, developers first need to understand the basic concepts and capabilities of Service Workers. Service Workers operate as event-driven scripts that can intercept and handle network requests made by the browser. They run independently of the main browser thread, allowing them to perform tasks like caching responses from the server and serving them to the application when offline.

One of the primary use cases for Service Workers in AJAX applications is offline caching. By caching static assets, such as HTML, CSS, JavaScript, and images, developers can ensure that users can still access the application's core functionality even when they're offline. To implement offline caching with Service Workers, developers use the **CacheStorage** API to store resources in a cache during the installation phase of the Service Worker. This cached content can then be retrieved and served to the application's UI when the user is offline.

Another essential feature of Service Workers is network interception, which allows them to intercept requests made by the application and respond with cached content when available. This feature is particularly useful for AJAX applications, as it ensures that users can still access dynamic content, such as API responses, even when offline. Developers can implement network interception in Service Workers by listening for fetch events and checking if the requested resource is available in the cache. If the resource is cached, the Service Worker can respond with the cached content; otherwise, it can pass the request to the network.

In addition to offline caching and network interception, Service Workers can also be used to implement background synchronization, allowing applications to sync data with the server when the user's device comes back online. This is especially useful for applications that rely on real-time data updates or user-generated content. To implement background synchronization with Service Workers, developers can listen for background sync events and trigger data synchronization tasks accordingly.

Deploying Service Workers for offline support in AJAX applications involves registering the Service Worker script with the application's HTML code. This can be done using the **navigator.serviceWorker.register()** method, which takes the path to the Service Worker script as an argument. Once registered, the Service Worker will be installed and activated the next time the application is loaded, enabling offline support and other features.

It's essential to consider the caching strategy when implementing Service Workers for offline support in AJAX applications. Developers should carefully choose which resources to cache and how long to cache them to ensure a balance between performance and data freshness. They should also implement cache invalidation strategies to ensure that cached content is updated when necessary and prevent stale data from being served to users.

Furthermore, developers should test their Service Worker implementation thoroughly to ensure that it behaves as expected in different network conditions and on various devices. This includes testing offline functionality, network interception, background synchronization, and cache management. By testing their Service Workers rigorously, developers can identify and address any issues or bugs before deploying them to production.

In summary, implementing Service Workers for offline support in AJAX applications is a powerful technique for enhancing the reliability and performance of web applications. By leveraging features like offline caching, network interception, and background synchronization, developers can ensure that users can access content even when they're offline or experiencing poor network conditions. With careful planning and testing, Service Workers can significantly improve the user experience of AJAX applications, making them more resilient and accessible across different devices and network environments.

Chapter 6: Security Considerations in AJAX Architectures

Cross-Site Request Forgery (CSRF) is a prevalent security vulnerability that affects web applications, including those utilizing AJAX for asynchronous communication. CSRF occurs when a malicious actor tricks a user into performing an unintended action on a web application where they are authenticated. To mitigate CSRF attacks in AJAX applications, developers employ various protection mechanisms and best practices.

One fundamental CSRF protection technique is the use of anti-CSRF tokens. These tokens are unique identifiers generated by the server and embedded into forms or AJAX requests. When a user submits a form or performs an AJAX request, the server verifies the presence and correctness of the anti-CSRF token to ensure that the request is legitimate. To implement anti-CSRF tokens in AJAX applications, developers generate a token on the server side and include it in the response to the initial page load. Subsequent AJAX requests include this token in the request headers or body, allowing the server to validate the request's authenticity.

Another approach to CSRF protection in AJAX applications is to utilize the SameSite attribute for cookies. The SameSite attribute restricts the scope of cookies to prevent them from being sent in cross-site requests. By setting the SameSite attribute to "Strict" or "Lax" for session cookies, developers can mitigate the risk of CSRF attacks by ensuring that cookies are not sent in cross-origin AJAX requests. Additionally, developers can use the "HttpOnly" attribute to prevent client-side scripts from accessing cookies, further enhancing the security of AJAX applications.

In addition to anti-CSRF tokens and SameSite cookies, developers can implement additional security measures such as origin validation and custom request headers. Origin validation involves verifying that AJAX requests originate from trusted domains or origins, thereby preventing malicious actors from forging requests from unauthorized sources. Custom request headers, such as the "X-Requested-With" header, can also be used to identify AJAX requests and differentiate them from other types of requests. By validating origin and request headers, developers can further enhance the security of their AJAX applications and protect against CSRF attacks.

Furthermore, developers should ensure that their AJAX endpoints are properly authenticated and authorized to prevent unauthorized access and mitigate the risk of CSRF attacks. This involves implementing robust authentication mechanisms, such as session management and OAuth tokens, and enforcing access control policies to restrict access to sensitive resources. By following the principle of least privilege and limiting the scope of user permissions, developers can minimize the potential impact of CSRF attacks and reduce the attack surface of their AJAX applications.

It's also essential for developers to stay informed about emerging security threats and best practices for securing AJAX applications. This includes keeping up-to-date with security advisories, vulnerability disclosures, and industry guidelines from organizations such as OWASP (Open Web Application Security Project). By staying vigilant and proactive, developers can identify and address security vulnerabilities in their AJAX applications before they can be exploited by malicious actors.

In summary, CSRF protection is a critical consideration for developers building AJAX applications, as these applications are susceptible to CSRF attacks due to their asynchronous nature. By implementing anti-CSRF tokens, utilizing SameSite cookies, validating origin and request headers, and enforcing robust authentication and authorization mechanisms, developers can effectively mitigate the risk of CSRF attacks and protect the integrity and security of their AJAX applications. Additionally, staying informed about emerging security threats and best practices is essential for maintaining the security posture of AJAX applications and defending against evolving threats.

Content Security Policy (CSP) is a crucial security mechanism designed to mitigate various types of attacks, including cross-site scripting (XSS), data injection, and clickjacking, by providing a set of directives that control the resources a web page is allowed to load. When it comes to AJAX (Asynchronous JavaScript and XML) applications, implementing CSP becomes even more critical due to the dynamic nature of content loading and the potential risks associated with fetching and executing remote resources.

To deploy CSP for AJAX applications effectively, developers need to understand the core concepts of CSP and how to tailor its directives to suit the requirements of their applications. One of the primary directives in CSP is the "script-src" directive, which controls the sources from which scripts can be loaded and executed. By specifying trusted sources for scripts, developers can prevent malicious scripts from being injected into their applications via AJAX requests.

For example, suppose an AJAX application fetches JavaScript code from a remote server to dynamically update its functionality. In that case, developers can use the "script-src" directive to whitelist specific domains from which scripts are allowed to be loaded. This can be achieved by configuring the CSP header in the server's response to include the appropriate directives.

cssCopy code

Header set Content-Security-Policy "script-src 'self' https://trusted-domain.com;"

In this example, the CSP header instructs the browser to only execute scripts that originate from the same domain as the application ("self") or from the trusted domain "https://trusted-domain.com." This helps prevent XSS attacks by restricting the execution of scripts to trusted sources.

Another essential directive in CSP for AJAX applications is the "connect-src" directive, which governs the sources from which the application can initiate network connections, such as AJAX requests. By specifying trusted domains for network connections, developers can prevent data exfiltration and unauthorized access to sensitive resources.

cssCopy code

Header set Content-Security-Policy "connect-src 'self' https://api.example.com;"

In this example, the "connect-src" directive allows AJAX requests to be made to the same origin ("self") or to the trusted domain "https://api.example.com." This ensures that AJAX requests are restricted to authorized endpoints, reducing the risk of data leakage and unauthorized access.

Additionally, developers can leverage other CSP directives such as "img-src," "style-src," and "font-src" to control the loading of images, stylesheets, and fonts in AJAX applications. By specifying trusted sources for these resources, developers can further enhance the security of their applications and mitigate the risk of various types of attacks.

Furthermore, CSP supports the use of nonces and hashes to enable inline scripts and styles while maintaining security. Developers can generate unique nonces or hashes for inline scripts and styles and include them in the CSP header to allow their execution. This approach helps prevent XSS attacks by ensuring that only authorized inline scripts and styles are executed by the browser.

cssCopy code

```
Header set Content-Security-Policy "script-src 'nonce-abc123' 'sha256-12345...';"
```

In this example, the CSP header includes a nonce ("abc123") and a SHA-256 hash of an inline script, allowing scripts with matching nonces or hashes to be executed by the browser.

Additionally, developers should consider implementing the "report-uri" directive in CSP to receive violation reports from the browser when a CSP policy is violated. These reports provide valuable insights into potential security vulnerabilities in AJAX applications, allowing developers to take proactive measures to address them.

arduinoCopy code

```
Header set Content-Security-Policy "report-uri /csp-report-endpoint;"
```

In this example, the CSP header specifies a report URI ("/csp-report-endpoint") where violation reports will be sent by the browser. Developers can then analyze these reports and take appropriate actions to rectify security issues in their applications.

Overall, implementing CSP for AJAX applications is essential for enhancing security and mitigating the risk of various types of attacks. By leveraging CSP directives effectively, developers can control the loading of remote resources, prevent XSS attacks, and safeguard sensitive data in their applications. Additionally, monitoring and analyzing violation reports can help developers identify and address security vulnerabilities, ensuring the continued integrity and security of their AJAX applications.

Chapter 7: Implementing Offline Capabilities with AJAX

Caching strategies play a pivotal role in enabling offline support for AJAX (Asynchronous JavaScript and XML) applications, ensuring seamless user experiences even when the network connection is unavailable or unreliable. By intelligently caching resources, such as HTML, CSS, JavaScript, and data, developers can mitigate the impact of network failures and provide users with uninterrupted access to critical application functionalities.

One of the most common caching strategies for offline support in AJAX applications is the use of service workers. Service workers are JavaScript files that run in the background of web browsers, intercepting network requests and enabling developers to control how resources are cached and served. By implementing service workers, developers can create robust offline experiences by precaching essential resources, caching dynamically fetched data, and serving cached content when the network is unavailable.

To deploy service workers for caching in an AJAX application, developers need to create a service worker JavaScript file and register it in the application's HTML files. The service worker can then be configured to cache specific resources using various caching strategies, such as cache-first, network-first, or stale-while-revalidate. These strategies determine how the service worker responds to network requests and whether it serves cached content or fetches resources from the network.

For example, to implement a cache-first strategy for static resources like HTML, CSS, and JavaScript files, developers can configure the service worker to intercept requests for these resources and serve them from the cache if available, falling back to the network only if the resource is not cached.

javascriptCopy code

```
// service-worker.js self.addEventListener('fetch',
function(event) { event.respondWith(
caches.match(event.request).then(function(respon
se) { return response || fetch(event.request); }) );
});
```

In this example, the service worker intercepts fetch events and attempts to match the requested resource with items in the cache. If a cached response is found, it is returned to the browser; otherwise, the request is forwarded to the network.

Another caching strategy commonly used in AJAX applications is the network-first strategy, where resources are fetched from the network by default but served from the cache if the network request fails or times out. This strategy ensures that users have access to the latest data whenever possible but still provides offline access to previously cached content.

javascriptCopy code

```
// service-worker.js self.addEventListener('fetch', function(event) { event.respondWith( fetch(event.request).catch(function() { return caches.match(event.request); }) ); });
```

In this example, the service worker attempts to fetch the requested resource from the network but falls back to the cache if the network request fails. This allows the application to continue functioning offline by serving cached content when the network is unavailable.

Additionally, developers can implement strategies like stale-while-revalidate to serve stale content from the cache while asynchronously fetching updated content from the network in the background. This approach minimizes the impact of network latency on user experiences and ensures that users always have access to the most up-to-date content whenever possible.

javascriptCopy code

```
// service-worker.js self.addEventListener('fetch', function(event) { event.respondWith( caches.open('dynamic-cache').then(function(cache) { return cache.match(event.request).then(function(response) { var fetchPromise =
```

```
fetch (event. request). then (function (networkRespon
se )                  {                  cache. put (event. request,
networkResponse. clone ());                                    return
networkResponse;     });    return    response    ||
fetchPromise; }); }) ); });
```

In this example, the service worker attempts to serve the requested resource from the cache but simultaneously fetches the resource from the network. If the resource is found in the cache, it is returned to the browser immediately, while the network request is made in the background to update the cache with the latest content.

Overall, caching strategies are essential for enabling offline support in AJAX applications, allowing developers to provide seamless user experiences even in challenging network conditions. By leveraging service workers and implementing caching strategies tailored to their application's requirements, developers can ensure that users have access to critical resources and functionalities regardless of network connectivity.

Background sync is a powerful technique for enabling offline data syncing in AJAX applications, ensuring that data updates made by users while offline are seamlessly synchronized with the server when the network connection is restored. This feature allows applications to provide a consistent user experience by allowing users to interact with data even when they are not connected to the internet. By leveraging background sync, developers can enhance the reliability and usability of AJAX applications, making them more resilient to network failures and improving user satisfaction.

To implement background sync in an AJAX application, developers can use the Background Sync API, which is supported by modern web browsers. This API allows developers to register a sync event that is triggered by the browser when certain conditions are met, such as when the device reconnects to the internet. When the sync event is fired, the browser executes a specified synchronization task, enabling developers to send pending data updates to the server.

The first step in implementing background sync is to register a sync event in the service worker script. This is done using the **registerSync()** method, which takes the name of the sync event and an options object as parameters. For example:

javascriptCopy code

```
// service-worker.js self.addEventListener('sync',
function(event) { if (event.tag === 'syncData') {
event.waitUntil(syncData()); } }); function
syncData() { // Perform data synchronization logic
here }
```

In this example, the service worker listens for sync events with the tag **'syncData'** and calls the **syncData()** function when such an event is fired.

Next, developers need to trigger the sync event when data updates are made while the application is offline. This can be done by using the **registerSync()** method in conjunction with other APIs, such as the IndexedDB API for client-side storage. For example:

javascriptCopy code

```
// app.js function saveDataLocally(data) { return
new Promise((resolve, reject) => { // Save data to
IndexedDB or other client-side storage // Resolve the
promise when data is saved successfully }); } function
sendDataToServer(data) { // Send data to the server
using AJAX or Fetch API } function
saveAndSyncData(data) { saveDataLocally(data)
.then(() => { if ('serviceWorker' in navigator &&
'SyncManager' in window) {
navigator.serviceWorker.ready.then(registration =>
{ registration.sync.register('syncData'); }); } else { //
Fallback logic for browsers that do not support
background sync sendDataToServer(data); } })
.catch(error => { console.error('Error saving data
locally:', error); }); }
```

In this example, the **saveAndSyncData()** function saves data to the client-side storage and triggers a sync event using the Background Sync API if the browser supports it. If background sync is not supported, the data is sent to the server immediately. Once the sync event is triggered, the service worker executes the **syncData()** function, which contains the

278

logic for synchronizing data with the server. This may involve retrieving pending data updates from the client-side storage and sending them to the server using AJAX or Fetch API calls.

javascriptCopy code

```
// service-worker.js function syncData() { return
new Promise((resolve, reject) => { // Retrieve
pending data updates from client-side storage //
Send data to the server using AJAX or Fetch API //
Resolve the promise when synchronization is
complete }); }
```

By implementing background sync in this manner, developers can ensure that data updates made by users while offline are synchronized with the server as soon as the network connection is restored. This helps to maintain data consistency across client and server, providing users with a seamless and reliable experience.

In addition to improving data synchronization, background sync also helps to conserve battery life and reduce bandwidth usage by batching data updates and synchronizing them only when a reliable network connection is available. This can lead to significant performance improvements, especially on mobile devices with limited resources.

Overall, background sync is a valuable technique for enabling offline data syncing in AJAX applications, allowing developers to create robust and reliable user experiences that work seamlessly regardless of network conditions. By leveraging the Background Sync API and integrating it with client-side storage and server-side APIs, developers can ensure that data updates are synchronized efficiently and effectively, improving the overall usability and reliability of their applications.

Chapter 8: Cross-Platform Compatibility in AJAX Solutions

Universal JavaScript techniques play a pivotal role in developing cross-platform AJAX applications, ensuring consistent behavior and user experience across different environments. In today's diverse ecosystem of web browsers, devices, and platforms, creating applications that function seamlessly across various contexts is crucial for reaching a wide audience and providing a consistent experience to users. Universal JavaScript, also known as Isomorphic JavaScript, enables developers to write code that can be executed both on the client and server sides, thereby facilitating the development of cross-platform AJAX applications.

One of the primary advantages of using universal JavaScript for cross-platform AJAX development is the ability to share code between the client and server environments. This allows developers to reuse business logic, data manipulation, and rendering code across different parts of the application, reducing duplication and promoting maintainability. By writing code that can be executed in both environments, developers can ensure consistency in behavior and avoid inconsistencies that may arise from executing code in different contexts.

To deploy universal JavaScript techniques in cross-platform AJAX applications, developers typically utilize frameworks and libraries that support server-side rendering, such as Next.js, Nuxt.js, or Angular Universal. These frameworks provide tools and utilities for building applications that can render content on the server and then hydrate it on the client, ensuring that the initial page load is fast and that subsequent interactions are smooth and responsive.

For example, in a Next.js application, developers can create pages using React components and define server-side rendering behavior by implementing a **getServerSideProps** function that fetches data from an API endpoint and passes it as props to the component. This allows the page to be pre-rendered on the server with the necessary data, improving performance and enabling search engine optimization.

javascriptCopy code

```javascript
// pages/index.js import axios from 'axios'; export async function getServerSideProps() { // Fetch data from API endpoint const response = await axios.get('https://api.example.com/data'); const data = response.data; // Return data as props return { props: { data } }; } function HomePage({ data }) { // Render page using data return ( <div> <h1>Universal JavaScript Techniques</h1> <p>{data}</p> </div> ); } export default HomePage;
```

In this example, the **getServerSideProps** function is used to fetch data from an API endpoint and pass it as props to the **HomePage** component. When the page is requested, Next.js pre-renders it on the server with the fetched data, ensuring that the content is available immediately and improving performance.

On the client side, the same React components can be used to hydrate the pre-rendered content, enabling client-side interactions and dynamic updates without reloading the page. This ensures a consistent user experience across different environments and devices, as the same code is executed on both the client and server sides.

By adopting universal JavaScript techniques for cross-platform AJAX development, developers can create applications that are fast, responsive, and accessible across a wide range of devices and platforms. By sharing code between the client and server environments, developers can streamline development workflows, improve code maintainability, and deliver a consistent user experience to users, regardless of their chosen platform or device.

Testing and debugging are essential aspects of developing cross-platform AJAX applications, ensuring their reliability, performance, and functionality across various devices, browsers, and environments. With the increasing complexity of web applications and the diversity of platforms they support, robust testing and debugging practices are crucial for identifying and resolving issues before they impact users.

One common approach to testing cross-platform AJAX applications is using automated testing frameworks and tools to validate their behavior and functionality. These tools enable developers to write test cases that simulate user interactions, API requests, and other scenarios, allowing them to verify that the application behaves as expected in different situations.

One popular testing framework for JavaScript applications is Jest, which provides a simple and intuitive interface for writing and running tests. To install Jest in a project, developers can use npm, a package manager for JavaScript:

bashCopy code

npm install --save-dev jest

Once Jest is installed, developers can create test files with the **.test.js** extension and write test cases using Jest's API. For example, to test a function that performs an AJAX request and returns data, developers can use Jest's mocking capabilities to simulate the AJAX call and verify the function's behavior:

javascriptCopy code

```
// api.js import axios from 'axios'; export async function fetchData() { const response = await axios.get('/api/data'); return response.data; }
```

javascriptCopy code

```
// api.test.js import { fetchData } from './api';
import axios from 'axios'; jest.mock('axios');
test('fetchData returns the correct data', async () =>
{ const data = { message: 'Hello, world!' };
axios.get.mockResolvedValue({ data }); const result
= await fetchData(); expect(result).toEqual(data);
});
```

In this example, Jest is used to test the **fetchData** function, which performs an AJAX request using Axios. By mocking the Axios library using Jest's **mock** function, developers can control the behavior of the AJAX call and ensure that the function behaves as expected.

In addition to unit testing individual functions and modules, developers can also perform integration testing to validate the interactions between different parts of the application, including AJAX requests, UI components, and state management. Integration testing frameworks like Cypress or Selenium WebDriver enable developers to automate browser interactions and simulate user behavior, allowing them to test the application's functionality in a real-world environment.

To use Cypress for integration testing, developers can install it via npm:

bashCopy code

npm install --save-dev cypress

Once Cypress is installed, developers can write test scripts using its API and run them in a headless browser or in interactive mode. For example, to test the behavior of a form submission using AJAX, developers can write a Cypress test case that interacts with the form elements and verifies that the AJAX request is sent correctly:

javascriptCopy code

```
// cypress/integration/form.spec.js describe('Form submission', () => { it('Submits the form via AJAX', () => { cy.visit('/');
cy.get('input[name="username"]').type('testuser');
cy.get('input[name="password"]').type('password');
cy.get('button[type="submit"]').click();
cy.intercept('POST', '/api/login').as('login');
cy.wait('@login').then((interception) => {
expect(interception.response.statusCode).to.equal(200);
expect(interception.response.body).to.have.property('token'); }); }); });
```

In this example, Cypress is used to test the submission of a login form via AJAX. The test script simulates user interactions with the form elements, clicks the submit button, and intercepts the AJAX request to validate its response.

In addition to automated testing, manual testing is also an essential part of the testing process, allowing developers to identify edge cases, usability issues, and performance bottlenecks that may not be caught by automated tests. Manual testing involves manually interacting with the application, exploring different features, and verifying its behavior in different scenarios.

To facilitate manual testing, developers can use browser developer tools to inspect network requests, view console logs, and debug JavaScript code. In Chrome DevTools, for example, developers can use the Network tab to monitor AJAX requests, the Console tab to view log messages and errors, and the Sources tab to debug JavaScript code.

By combining automated testing with manual testing and using tools like Jest, Cypress, and browser developer tools, developers can ensure the reliability, performance, and functionality of cross-platform AJAX applications, delivering a seamless and consistent user experience across different devices, browsers, and environments.

Chapter 9: Performance Tuning and Optimization in AJAX

Minification and compression are crucial techniques for optimizing the performance of AJAX applications, reducing file sizes and improving loading times. As modern web applications become more complex, with larger codebases and numerous dependencies, minimizing the size of JavaScript, CSS, and other assets is essential for enhancing user experience and reducing bandwidth usage.

Minification is the process of removing unnecessary characters, such as whitespace, comments, and formatting, from source code without altering its functionality. This results in smaller file sizes, making the code more efficient to transfer over the network and reducing the time it takes for the browser to parse and execute the code.

One common tool for minifying JavaScript code is UglifyJS, which can be installed via npm:

bashCopy code

```
npm install uglify-js --save-dev
```

Once installed, developers can use the UglifyJS CLI to minify JavaScript files:

bashCopy code

```
uglifyjs input.js -o output.min.js
```

This command takes an input JavaScript file (**input.js**) and minifies it, writing the minified output to

output.min.js. Developers can also specify additional options, such as enabling source map generation or specifying custom compression settings.

In addition to minifying JavaScript code, developers can also minify CSS and HTML files using tools like cssnano and html-minifier, respectively. These tools operate similarly to UglifyJS, removing unnecessary characters and optimizing the code for faster loading times.

Compression, on the other hand, involves reducing the size of files by encoding them using a more efficient encoding scheme, such as gzip or Brotli. Unlike minification, compression works at the network level, reducing the amount of data transferred between the server and the client.

Most web servers support compression out of the box, allowing developers to enable compression for static assets, including JavaScript, CSS, and HTML files. For example, in Apache HTTP Server, developers can enable gzip compression by adding the following configuration directives to the server's configuration file:

apacheCopy code

<IfModule mod_deflate.c> # Enable compression for CSS, JavaScript, and HTML files AddOutputFilterByType DEFLATE text/css application/javascript text/html # Optionally, specify additional file types to compress #

AddOutputFilterByType DEFLATE text/plain text/xml image/svg+xml </IfModule>

Similarly, in Nginx, developers can enable gzip compression by adding the following configuration directives to the server block:

nginxCopy code

gzip on; gzip_types text/plain text/css application/javascript text/xml application/xml application/xml+rss application/json;

These configuration directives instruct the web server to compress files with the specified MIME types using gzip compression before sending them to the client. This reduces the size of the files and improves loading times, especially for users with limited bandwidth or slower internet connections.

In addition to enabling compression at the server level, developers can also pre-compress static assets using tools like gzip or Brotli, storing the compressed files alongside the uncompressed versions. This allows the web server to serve the pre-compressed files directly to clients that support compression, further reducing latency and improving performance.

By combining minification and compression techniques, developers can significantly improve the performance of AJAX applications, reducing file sizes, optimizing network transfer times, and delivering a faster and more responsive user experience. These optimization techniques are essential for modern web development, particularly in the context of mobile devices and low-bandwidth environments, where performance is critical for user satisfaction and retention.

Lazy loading and code splitting are powerful techniques used in AJAX applications to improve performance by reducing initial load times and optimizing resource utilization. As modern web applications become more complex and feature-rich, loading all resources upfront can lead to longer initial load times and decreased user experience. Lazy loading and code splitting address this issue by loading resources only when they are needed, thus improving loading times and reducing unnecessary resource consumption.

Lazy loading involves deferring the loading of certain resources, such as images, scripts, or data, until they are required to be displayed or executed. This technique is particularly useful for optimizing the loading of large images, videos, or components that are not immediately visible on the initial page load.

One common scenario where lazy loading is used in AJAX applications is with images. Rather than loading all images on the page when it initially loads, images are loaded dynamically as the user scrolls down the page or when they come into view. This is achieved using JavaScript event listeners, such as the **scroll** event or Intersection Observer API, to detect when an image is about to enter the viewport and trigger its loading.

For example, in a React application, lazy loading of images can be implemented using the **React.lazy** function and the **Suspense** component:

javascriptCopy code

```
import React, { Suspense } from 'react'; const LazyImage = React.lazy(() => import('./LazyImage')); function MyComponent() { return ( <Suspense fallback={<div>Loading...</div>}> <LazyImage /> </Suspense> ); } export default MyComponent;
```

In this example, the **React.lazy** function is used to dynamically import the **LazyImage** component only when it is needed. The **Suspense** component provides a fallback UI to display while the component is being loaded asynchronously.

Similarly, code splitting involves breaking down a large JavaScript bundle into smaller, more manageable chunks, and loading them on demand. This is especially beneficial for large-scale applications with numerous features or pages, where loading the entire application code upfront would result in longer load times and increased resource consumption.

Webpack, a popular module bundler for JavaScript applications, provides built-in support for code splitting using dynamic imports. Developers can use dynamic import statements to split their code into separate bundles that are loaded asynchronously when needed.

javascriptCopy code

```
// Lazy load a module import('./module')
.then(module => { // Module is loaded })
.catch(error => { // Handle error });
```

In this example, the **import()** function is used to dynamically import a module. The module is loaded asynchronously, and a promise is returned that resolves once the module is loaded successfully.

By combining lazy loading and code splitting techniques, developers can significantly improve the performance of AJAX applications, reducing initial load times, optimizing resource utilization, and providing a smoother and more responsive user experience. These techniques are essential for modern web development, particularly for large-scale applications with complex user interfaces and feature sets.

Chapter 10: AJAX in the Era of Mobile Development

Mobile-first design principles are essential for creating modern AJAX applications that provide a seamless user experience across devices of varying screen sizes and resolutions. In today's digital landscape, where mobile usage continues to rise, prioritizing mobile-friendly design ensures that applications are accessible and user-friendly on smartphones, tablets, and other mobile devices.

At the core of mobile-first design is the principle of designing for the smallest screen size first, typically mobile phones, and then progressively enhancing the design for larger screens, such as tablets, laptops, and desktop computers. This approach prioritizes the needs of mobile users, who often have limited screen real estate and may be accessing the application on slower network connections.

One of the key benefits of mobile-first design is its focus on simplicity and usability. By starting with a minimalistic design optimized for smaller screens, developers can prioritize essential content and functionality, ensuring that users can quickly find what they need without unnecessary clutter or distractions. This minimalist approach not only improves the user experience on mobile devices but also translates well to larger screens, where the additional space can be used to enhance the layout and presentation of content.

To implement mobile-first design in AJAX applications, developers should adopt several best practices and techniques:

Responsive Layouts: Use CSS media queries to create responsive layouts that adapt to different screen sizes. Design flexible and fluid layouts that adjust dynamically based on the viewport size, ensuring that content remains readable and accessible on all devices.

Viewport Meta Tag: Include the viewport meta tag in the HTML document to control the initial scale and width of the viewport. This tag helps ensure that the application displays correctly on mobile devices by setting the viewport width to the device's width and disabling zooming.

htmlCopy code

```
<meta name="viewport" content="width=device-width, initial-scale=1">
```

Progressive Enhancement: Start with a basic design that works well on all devices, and then progressively enhance the design for larger screens by adding additional features and enhancements. This approach ensures that the application remains functional and accessible on older devices and browsers while taking advantage of advanced features on newer devices.

Touch-Friendly Interaction: Design interactive elements, such as buttons, links, and menus, to be touch-friendly and easy to use on touchscreens.

Increase the size of clickable areas and provide ample spacing between elements to prevent accidental taps and improve usability on mobile devices.

Optimized Performance: Prioritize performance optimization techniques, such as lazy loading of images and scripts, minification and compression of assets, and efficient resource caching, to ensure fast loading times and smooth performance on mobile devices with limited processing power and network connectivity.

User Feedback and Testing: Gather feedback from users and conduct usability testing on a variety of devices to identify any usability issues or pain points. Iterate on the design based on user feedback and testing results to improve the overall user experience.

By following these mobile-first design principles and techniques, developers can create AJAX applications that provide a seamless and intuitive user experience across devices, catering to the growing number of mobile users and ensuring that the application remains accessible and functional on all platforms. Mobile-first design is not just a best practice but a necessity in today's mobile-centric world, where users expect applications to be optimized for their devices and provide a consistent experience regardless of screen size or resolution.

Touch events and gesture recognition play a pivotal role in enhancing the user experience of mobile AJAX interfaces, providing intuitive ways for users to interact with content and navigate through applications on touchscreen devices. As smartphones and tablets continue to dominate the digital landscape, understanding how to leverage touch events and gesture recognition effectively is essential for creating engaging and user-friendly mobile experiences.

At the core of touch events are a series of events triggered by user interactions with the touchscreen, including tapping, swiping, pinching, and dragging. These touch events enable developers to capture user input and respond dynamically, allowing for a more interactive and immersive experience compared to traditional mouse-based interactions.

One of the most common touch events is the "touchstart" event, which occurs when the user places a finger on the touchscreen. This event is typically followed by "touchmove" events as the user drags their finger across the screen and "touchend" events when the user lifts their finger. By listening for these touch events, developers can implement a wide range of interactive features, such as scrolling, dragging elements, and triggering actions based on touch input.

```
javascriptCopy code
// Example of listening for touch events
element.addEventListener('touchstart',
function(event) { // Handle touchstart event });
element.addEventListener('touchmove',
```

```
function(event) { // Handle touchmove event });
element.addEventListener('touchend',
function(event) { // Handle touchend event });
```

Gesture recognition builds upon touch events by detecting specific patterns or combinations of touch input, such as pinch-to-zoom, swipe-to-navigate, and rotate-to-pan. These gestures provide intuitive ways for users to interact with content and perform common actions, such as zooming in on images, navigating through slideshows, and scrolling through lists.

To implement gesture recognition in mobile AJAX interfaces, developers can use specialized libraries and frameworks that provide pre-built gesture recognition functionality. One popular library for gesture recognition is Hammer.js, which offers a simple and flexible API for detecting and handling gestures across a wide range of devices and browsers.

bashCopy code

```
# Install Hammer.js using npm npm install hammerjs
```

javascriptCopy code

```
// Example of using Hammer.js for gesture
recognition var hammer = new Hammer(element);
hammer.on('swipe', function(event) { // Handle
swipe gesture }); hammer.on('pinch',
function(event) { // Handle pinch gesture });
```

In addition to touch events and gesture recognition, developers can also leverage device orientation and motion sensors, such as accelerometer and gyroscope, to create innovative and immersive mobile experiences. By detecting changes in device orientation and motion, developers can implement features like tilt-based navigation, shake-to-refresh, and motion-controlled games.

javascriptCopy code

```
// Example of using device orientation events
window.addEventListener('deviceorientation',
function(event) { // Handle device orientation
change }); // Example of using device motion events
window.addEventListener('devicemotion',
function(event) { // Handle device motion change });
```

However, it's essential to consider the limitations and constraints of touch events and gesture recognition, especially when designing for a wide range of devices and screen sizes. Not all devices support the same set of touch events and gestures, and user preferences and accessibility needs may vary. Therefore, developers should test their mobile AJAX interfaces across different devices and browsers to ensure consistent behavior and usability.

In summary, touch events and gesture recognition are powerful tools for creating engaging and intuitive mobile AJAX interfaces. By leveraging these technologies effectively and considering user needs and preferences, developers can deliver compelling mobile experiences that delight users and drive engagement.

Conclusion

In summary, the AJAX Programming book bundle offers a comprehensive journey through the world of asynchronous JavaScript and XML (AJAX), equipping readers with the knowledge and skills needed to develop powerful web and mobile applications. Throughout the four books included in this bundle, readers have explored various aspects of AJAX programming, starting from the fundamentals and progressing to intermediate and advanced techniques.

In Book 1, "AJAX Programming for Beginners: Building Dynamic Web Interfaces," readers gained a solid understanding of AJAX fundamentals, including making asynchronous requests, handling responses, and updating web interfaces dynamically. With practical examples and step-by-step tutorials, beginners learned how to build interactive and responsive web applications using AJAX.

Moving on to Book 2, "Intermediate AJAX Techniques: Enhancing User Experience and Performance," readers delved deeper into AJAX techniques aimed at enhancing user experience and improving application performance. Topics such as error handling, caching strategies, and optimizing AJAX requests were explored, empowering developers to create faster and more efficient web applications.

In Book 3, "Advanced AJAX Strategies: Scalable Solutions for Complex Web Applications," readers were introduced to advanced AJAX concepts and strategies tailored for complex web applications. From managing concurrent requests to implementing server-side pagination and integrating AJAX with backend technologies, developers learned how to architect scalable and robust solutions for modern web applications.

Finally, Book 4, "Mastering AJAX: Architecting Robust Web and Mobile Solutions," provided readers with a comprehensive overview of advanced AJAX topics, including real-time updates, security considerations, and offline support. By mastering these advanced techniques, developers gained the expertise needed to architect sophisticated web and mobile solutions that meet the demands of today's dynamic and interconnected digital landscape.

Overall, the AJAX Programming book bundle equips developers of all levels with the essential knowledge and skills needed to harness the full potential of AJAX in their web and mobile applications. Whether you're a beginner looking to build dynamic web interfaces or an experienced developer seeking to master advanced AJAX strategies, this book bundle offers a comprehensive and practical guide to AJAX programming. With the knowledge gained from these books, readers are well-positioned to create powerful, responsive, and scalable applications that deliver exceptional user experiences across various platforms and devices.

www.ingramcontent.com/pod-product-compliance
Lightning Source LLC
Chambersburg PA
CBHW070935050326
40689CB00014B/3207